WISDOM
of the
ANCIENTS

www.penguin.co.uk

For more information on Neil Oliver and his books,
see his website at www.neiloliver.com

WISDOM

of the

ANCIENTS

LIFE LESSONS FROM OUR DISTANT PAST

NEIL OLIVER

BANTAM PRESS

TRANSWORLD PUBLISHERS
Penguin Random House, One Embassy Gardens, 8 Viaduct Gardens, London SW11 7BW
www.penguin.co.uk

Transworld is part of the Penguin Random House group of companies
whose addresses can be found at global.penguinrandomhouse.com

First published in Great Britain in 2020 by Bantam Press
an imprint of Transworld Publishers

Lines from W. H. Auden and Louis MacNeice, 'Their Last Will and Testament',
from *Letters from Iceland* (Faber & Faber Ltd, 2018) © W. H. Auden and Louis MacNeice.
Lines from Seamus Heaney, 'Bogland', from *Door into the Dark* (Faber & Faber Ltd, 2018)
© Seamus Heaney. Lines from Hilaire Belloc, *The Old Road: From Canterbury to Winchester*
(Constable and Company, 1911), reprinted by permission of PFD on behalf of:
The Estate of Hilaire Belloc © The Estate of Hilaire Belloc

Every effort has been made to obtain the necessary permissions with
reference to copyright material, both illustrative and quoted. We apologize
for any omissions in this respect and will be pleased to make the
appropriate acknowledgements in any future edition.

A CIP catalogue record for this book
is available from the British Library.

ISBN 9781787633094

Typeset in 10.75/15 pt Minion Pro by Jouve (UK), Milton Keynes
Printed and bound in Great Britain by Clays Ltd, Elcograf S.p.A.

Penguin Random House is committed to a sustainable
future for our business, our readers and our planet. This book
is made from Forest Stewardship Council® certified paper.

To my dad
Archibald Paterson Oliver
Older and wiser
All my love

Contents

CONTENTS

CHAPTER TIMELINE

TIMELINE *of* WORLD HISTORY

AD 2016	UK votes to leave the European Union
2012	World population reaches 7 billion
1973	UK joins the European Common Market
1960	World population reaches 3 billion
1947	Partition of India
1939–45	Second World War
1927	World population reaches 2 billion
1914–18	First World War

1800– WORLD POPULATION REACHES 1 BILLION

1776	American Declaration of Independence
1707	Parliaments of England and Scotland united
1603	Crowns of England and Scotland united
1492	Columbus in the New World
1428	Founding of Aztec Empire
eleventh century	Founding of Great Zimbabwe in Africa
1066	Battle of Hastings and the Norman Conquest
793	Vikings attack Lindisfarne, England
597	Augustine's Christian mission to England
570	Birth of Muhammad
563	Columba on Iona, Scotland
476	Fall of Roman Empire in the west
410	Sack of Rome and beginning of Roman withdrawal from Britain
324	Byzantium becomes new capital of Roman Empire
43	Roman conquest of Britannia

BIRTH OF CHRIST

30 BC	Death of Cleopatra, in Alexandria, Egypt
44 BC	Murder of Julius Caesar
259 BC	Birth of Qin Shi Huang, first emperor of a unified China

323 BC	Death of Alexander the Great
fifth and fourth centuries BC	Classical Greece
509 BC–27 BC	Roman Republic
551 BC	Birth of Confucius, in China
563 BC (possible)	Birth of Buddha, in India
753 BC	Founding of City of Rome
970 BC	Solomon succeeds David as King of Israel
1200 BC	Rise of Ancient Greece
1342 BC	Birth of Tutankhamun in Egypt
2600–2500 BC	Fourth Dynasty of Ancient Egypt: the pyramid-building age
2850–2200 BC	Building of Avebury Stone Circle
3200 BC	Ness of Brodgar on Orkney, Newgrange and Knowth in Ireland
4000 BC	Horses domesticated on Eurasian steppes
5500 BC	Copper smelting in Europe
9000 BC	Permanent settlement at Jericho
9000 BC	Construction of ritual centre at Göbekli Tepe, in Turkey
9000 BC	Advent of farming in Near East
12,000 years ago	End of last ice age in Europe, and extinction of the mammoth
16,000 years ago	*Homo sapiens* in the Americas
25,000–15,000 years ago	Last ice age at maximum extent in Europe
34,000 years ago	Earliest *Homo sapiens* in British Isles, Paviland, South Wales
60,000 years ago	*Homo sapiens* in Australia
80,000 years ago	*Homo sapiens* migrate out of Africa into Europe and Asia
300,000 years ago	*Homo neanderthalensis* in Europe
500,000 years ago	*Homo heidelbergensis* in West Sussex, England
950,000 years ago	*Homo antecessor* in Norfolk, England
2 million years ago	*Homo erectus* in Africa
3.7 million years ago	*Australopithecus afarensis* in Africa

Introduction

The real problem of humanity is the following:
we have palaeolithic emotions, medieval institutions
and God-like technology.

– E. O. WILSON,
in *Harvard Magazine* (2009)

I WROTE THIS BOOK in search of answers – and if not answers then in the hope I would find reassurance and reasons for optimism. Our world now seems especially bad-tempered. Temperatures are rising. The news is often doom-laden and filled with hopelessness. But among the apocalyptic prophecies are the words of a few commentators claiming quite the contrary – that in all of recorded history this is the best time to be alive: fewer people in poverty, more food, better living conditions, increased life expectancy, the boundless potential of modern medicine and technology. I read it all – the forewarnings of the end of the world side by side with the insistence we've never had it so good – and I am filled with doubt and uncertainty about who and what to believe. What to do for the best? For all we have in the modern world, all we have gained by this point in time, simple peace of mind is hard to find. In search of that elusive treasure, I have looked back at the world of our ancestors.

Edward Osborne Wilson is an American biologist. His specialism has been the study of ant society but his line above about humanity's palaeolithic emotions resting uneasily alongside God-like technology resonates strongly with me. Humans of one sort or another have been around for at least four million years. For most of that time our ancestors were hunters. A few decades of internal combustion engines, penicillin and smartphones have not changed our essential nature. It seems fair to say that even now in the twenty-first century our brains are still running on hunter software. In the last 10,000 years we have learned all sorts of tricks – farming, writing, city-living, mechanized industry, manned flight, rockets, computers, the internet – but as hunters we are always looking for more, something else, things we need and that we might make use of. We can't help looking, hunting.

Over the last few centuries a tiny minority of men and women have learned to think like scientists, and it is scientific thinking that has enabled all the wondrous advances that have made possible the modern world, and improved the lives of billions of people. But in spite of all those steps forward, the western world is home to many unhappy people – depressed, stressed, lonely, self-loathing, self-doubting, even hopeless and nihilistic. Scientists have explained much of the what, how, where and when of the universe, but what science cannot do – or has not done so far – is tell us how to be alive in the world . . . *why* to be alive in the world. Science tells us what life is, not what it is for. Whether or not the answers even exist we seem to need to ask the questions. It might matter to look for them as much as to find them.

Most of us are not full-time scientists. Even those who have been trained to think like scientists are able to sustain the effort required for only short periods. For the rest of the time they think like us. Our hunter ancestors were not scientists but it seems they sought answers – answers to questions about what it meant to be human and alive. Long before there was science there were stories to explain the experience of life. Different people in different places, though separated by vast distances as well as by time, somehow came up with variations of the same stories and told them to their children – tales about the creation of the world, the separation of land, sea and sky, the making of the first people, the coming of floods, the vengeance of gods and the adventures of heroes. The oldest stories, those that have lasted longest, might simply be a consequence of being alive, occurring spontaneously in our consciousness, like crystals in liquid. Or else they were the product of hundreds of thousands of years of lives lived, observations of what worked and what helped.

It seems our species has a need for stories. After a long time stories are spun like wool into threads and then woven into mythology, belief and religions. A mythology is a fine thing – like the stories told within families about their own private pasts. Some of those family stories are true, others less so, but all of them matter. Remembered and retold, they remind family members about things they might otherwise forget. Stories are threads of the weave that holds each of them in place within the family, and the family within the universe.

Because I cannot think like a scientist I have always needed stories to help me understand complex ideas. I have opened and begun numerous books on quantum theory but the maths has always got in the way. Maths is the language nature speaks, but I don't. The American physicist Nick Herbert observed that the old Newtonian model described the universe in terms of big things made of small things, small things made of smaller things, and so on. According to QT, he said, the universe is more like an amorphous cloud of possibilities and probabilities in which entities behave one way while they are observed, and in other ways when they are not observed. Then he delivers a line of storytelling that allows me to understand. He says we humans exist in 'a King Midas-like predicament', unable ever to feel the true texture of reality because everything we touch turns, in that moment of our touching it, into solid matter. I get that, or at least I glimpse his meaning out of the corner of my eye. Albert Einstein explained relativity by saying that a young man who had to press his hand against a red-hot stove for five seconds would experience that packet of time differently from five seconds spent with a beautiful young woman sat in his lap. I get that too. Stories are wisdom distilled, the essence of all that is important.

In *Slaughterhouse-Five*, American author Kurt Vonnegut told a story that let me see that our human view of time and the universe might only be a consequence of our finite existence. His anti-hero is Billy Pilgrim, a Second World War soldier in the US army abducted from Earth by aliens from the planet Tralfamadore. Billy finds that rather than a linear, unfolding process – birth, life, death – Tralfamadorians see every thing and every time together, all at once:

> Billy Pilgrim says that the Universe does not look like a lot of bright little dots to the creatures from Tralfamadore. The creatures can see where each star has been and where it is going, so that the heavens are filled with rarefied, luminous spaghetti. And Tralfamadorians don't see human beings as two-legged creatures, either. They see them as great millipedes – 'with babies' legs at one end and old people's legs at the other'.

Stories like this enable me to see better.

In his novel *The Go-Between*, L. P. Hartley remarked that the past is a foreign country, 'they do things differently there'. The world of the ancients is not ours, and some of their behaviours and practices appear outlandish and alien. Still, they have a great deal to tell us if we are ready to pay attention.

I was drawn to history out of a (forlorn) wish to start the story of humankind at the beginning. This is an impossible dream. History is a story without a beginning. The beginning of the story of humankind is always out of reach. And so I became an archaeologist in the hope of at least getting closer to the always-elusive page one of the book.

While I am impressed by what we have become by way of science, I have taken solace in what we used to be, how we used to think. This is not about wanting to go back to the world we came from (spare me always from any world without anaesthetic and modern dentistry) but because I dream of that DNA of the first of us, coiled and sleeping in the twisted helix of our own, and what memories it might yield.

Between the last two ice ages, a few tens of thousands of years ago, the first of our kind arrived in Europe – the original marque, maybe the best of us, Cro-Magnon. They made lives in a world of rhinos and cave lions, bears and bison, giant aurochs, and a deer called megaloceros that stood 7 feet tall at the shoulder and had antlers so wide a family might have sheltered under them if they dared. Their lives were physically hard, their world filled with lethal danger. Nonetheless they coped and lived long enough to make the people who made us. Everything they needed they made. Everything they ate they caught and killed or searched for. Every fire that warmed them was kindled from dry sticks with clever hands. The experience of that world, lives lived across thousands of years, provided the time for learning many lessons.

Humankind's oldest memories are stories handed down for a length of time impossible to measure. In the beginning they were only spoken. Between 4,000 and 5,000 years ago our species learned to write. Some time after picking up that trick – snatching thoughts from the air like butterflies and pinning them to a board – some stories were committed to wet clay and then to the page. Assume the stories that have lasted, that were remembered and made permanent, were important, containing hard-won knowledge about how to live a life. Those stories with their dusty, iridescent wings are the fragile flutterings of understanding.

Maybe the old stories we have are just chance survivals – lucky fossils made safe against the rising tide of time that washed everything else away. Or they were remembered because of the words alone, cherished for their rhythms and cadences. Random legacy or not, those oldest stories are fossils of our own past lives.

In that world before writing, before stories were written down and preserved, human emotions are difficult to locate. Time has edited the past, deleting scenes. The feelings and passions of our ancestors are hard to see among stones and bones, and yet it is those emotions that we have in common. It makes sense to me that it is at least possible that we might be helped in our time and world by seeing how they coped in theirs. So much has changed between their time and ours, but human emotions are surely the same. What was felt in their world is felt in ours.

In life we eventually reach the edge of our understanding, but we know reality has not run out at that point. There is more to see. There are leaps of the imagination that we might attempt, in the hope of glimpsing the world, and life, as the ancients saw it. Archaeology and history offer such glimpses – of sadness as well as of happiness, and other emotions besides. We might take comfort from being reminded about what has remained constant for thousands of years. When ancient places and things are revisited – graves, works of art, surrendered treasures – it might be possible to see them for what they are: human emotions, good and bad, made manifest. I have tried to splice some together here, like out-takes joined together once more and with a bright light shone through them.

As technology speeds our progress into the future, it feels as though our separation from the world of the past is accelerating. The past is getting ever smaller in the rearview mirror. Even the world I grew up in is melting, receding. This is normal and inevitable but I am amazed by how much my childhood world seems antique to me. It is a measure of how fast times change, how quickly experience is lost. I was born in 1967. I am fifty-three this year and my early memories feel remote and dusty. I remember a house before central heating, dotted with little islands of warmth provided by paraffin heaters. I remember ice on the inside of windows. I remember having to switch on the TV set – and we called it the TV *set* – five minutes before we wanted to watch anything. This was to let the valves warm up. The TV set in question transmitted only in black and white. Before I left the house my mum would check that I had a two-pence piece in my pocket in case I needed to use a phone box. We moved from that house when I was six or seven but I still remember the phone number: 60832. Mum had me and my sisters memorize it in case we needed to call home in an emergency. I remember when fresh orange juice was a starter in restaurants, served in a shot glass delivered on a saucer. I remember electric vehicles the first time round, in the form of the milk float that delivered our milk in glass bottles that were endlessly recycled. Talk about green. I remember the whispering of its tyres on the tarmac. Direct memories of that time, just half a century ago, will be lost with the death of my generation. Any lessons they might offer will drift closer to oblivion.

I think about the changes my dad's dad lived to see during the course of his ninety-plus years. He was born into a horse-drawn Victorian world and fought on the Somme, and at Passchendaele. Later he watched a man walk on the moon (on a black and white TV, obviously), the space shuttle and the rise of computers. In *The Structure of Scientific Revolutions*, American science philosopher Thomas Kuhn coined the term 'paradigm shift', by which he meant those advances that are great enough, revolutionary enough, to leave us with no option but to see and understand things differently. Things might still look the same, but our appreciation of them is altered. That alteration is no bad thing, but all perspectives are of value. Having the new need not involve losing the old. Grandpa was born into a world still in thrall to Newton's understanding of the way things are (or rather were). By the time Grandpa was in his teens, German physicists Max Planck and Albert Einstein had walked humanity into the universe of relativity and quantum theory. The universe was as it had always been, but we were taught to see it differently. Planck and Einstein were standing on the shoulders of giants – Michael Faraday, James Clerk Maxwell and others – but it was a paradigm shift, and all the mind-bending technologies we take for granted are the direct or indirect result of that leap.

In my lifetime, which overlapped with Grandpa's until I was nineteen, we have continued to hurtle ahead. In spite of the speed, and the distance travelled, we remain connected to the most distant past, by what Abraham Lincoln called 'the mystic chords of memory'. In my imagination I picture those chords reaching back through time for three and a half billion years to the beginning of life. This makes sense because our existence is dependent on myriad ancestors having managed to pass their inheritance down the line to us, through uncounted couplings. The mystic chords of our species' memory echo all the way back to an ancient world in which stories, old stories, were all we had for answers to all of our questions.

Intentionally or not, the advent of scientific thinking sounded the death-knell for the old answers. The birth of modern science provided the sharp axe with which we cut down the gnarled tree that had grown from stories, myth and religion. In the soil left fallow by its absence we have grown ideologies to tell us what to do with life. Every religion is also an ideology, but the secular ideologies planted in the nineteenth and twentieth centuries grew rapidly and, in the case of some, out of control. Fascism, communism . . . the death tolls of the old religions, achieved over centuries and millennia, were reached by the new ideologies in a matter of years. Here we are in the twenty-first century, shell-shocked and blinking after the horrors of the twentieth, and the people of the technological west are still in search of meaning. It feels sometimes that the need for meaning has grown stronger. Science keeps giving – more and more and faster and faster – but its gifts are not enough. Nowadays we are goaded into worrying and feeling impotent about a great deal. The world we have taken for granted is coming to an end, they say, and it is our own fault. On account of our thoughtlessness and selfishness, they say, we have summoned the flood, or winter everlasting, or both.

Happiness – which is, technically, the cessation of suffering, however brief – is elusive magic. Peace of mind might be easier to come by, and it may be found in the wisdom of those who went before. The lessons of the ancients are the distillation of millions of years of living, suffering, happiness and sadness.

Whatever happens, whatever the future holds, good or bad, we can try and remember something. Whatever happens, some of us will survive and keep going, or start over. What we choose to remember is up to us – to each of us as individuals as well as collectively as a civilization. If we have to leave in a hurry, travelling light, it is worth remembering that stories are easily carried, tucked away like seeds, lighter than seeds, which might be planted elsewhere. In the beginning was the word – which is to say that words are the shattered fragments of what once was whole, the whole story, and from which we might assemble anything at all. Words are a gift of incalculable value.

Here is my pocketful of seeds. They are slight, easily overlooked. From them I have learned things that matter to me, things I believe worthy of remembrance, simple things that say something to me about how to be alive, and also why.

1.

Earth

Callanish
and the rock of ages

Remembering speechlessly we seek the great
forgotten language, the lost lane-end into heaven,
a stone, a leaf, an unfound door.

— THOMAS WOLFE,
Look Homeward, Angel

To try to make sense of what is going on, I like to search for the beginning of things, to start with something I can hold on to, and refer back to.

Before the beginning, say scientists, there was absence. In the beginning, in a place unknown, appeared a point immeasurably small. For reasons we understand imperfectly it began to expand, inflating like a puffball in the night. There was heat inside and also space and time, all the space and time there will ever be. Instead of absence there was all at once the potential for everything – all of it from within the point that had occupied no space at all. Until the expansion began there was no space and no time either. There had been no void. Instead there was less than that, less than nothing. When the expansion began, time began too. The clock started ticking.

I struggle with all of this, but I read and I listen and I have been taught to trust what science teaches us.

Within the expanding space, temperatures of billions of degrees Celsius cooked into existence hydrogen and helium. Those elements would make up 99 per cent of the universe. It is not in the nature of the universe for matter and energy to be evenly spread, like butter over toast. Just as money and power find their ways into the pockets of the few, so the universe prefers vast swatches of nothingness randomly dotted with the priceless jewels that are bright stars. Almost all of the universe is poor, empty pockets. A mere smidgen is blessed with any sort of warmth. 'To them that have, more shall be given, until they have an abundance,' wrote Matthew in his Gospel. 'From them that have not, even what little they have shall be taken away.' And so matter came together, helplessly and unavoidably, clumping to form stars and galaxies. Inside the hearts of the stars were cooked the rest of the elements. When those stars died the elements were freed to come together as everything else, including us.

The events of the Big Bang are new lore, a modern prayer for the muttering. Incomprehensible events, mystical in tone and yet common knowledge. The US television sitcom *The Big Bang Theory* even incorporates the basics into the lyrics of its theme song.

As recently as 2013 astronomers using the European Planck space telescope concluded, from their measurement of heat left over from the making of the universe, that the best figure for the age of it all was 13.8 billion years. In 2019, for an article in a publication called *Astrophysical Journal*, Nobel Laureate Adam Riess completed a set of measurements designed to corroborate that figure. Together with teams doing similar work elsewhere, Riess had observed and measured the radiation of stars scattered through the galaxies. To everyone's surprise their work suggested the universe might be a billion years younger (a *billion* years younger!) than they had thought – so maybe just 12.5 billion years old.

I read the results of these studies and do my best but I don't really comprehend. The most I glean from the maths, inscrutable as Sanskrit to me, is that our understanding sits on loose sand. How did we lose a billion years? Do you know how long it takes to count to a billion? Thirty-one years. We have no way of knowing how much we know, far less how much we do not.

Scientists have given Earth an age of 4.5 billion years – a third of that of the universe, give or take. For a billion years and more our home was boiling hot, more liquid than solid and with no outer crust; a glob of melting butter falling through forever. After all the billions of years since the infinitesimal point pricked the nothingness – nine billion? ten? – comes something a person might hold on to at last, even stand upon.

In that Hadean soup was conjured the rock geologists call Lewisian gneiss. Gneiss is a word with German roots. A person can put their weight behind a word like gneiss by sounding a hard 'g' (as in 'gold'), making the double 's' into 'shh', and finishing by clicking the tongue behind the teeth to make a 't' that is almost a 'tut'. G-nysh-T. However you say it – G-nysh-T, or 'nice' – the name means something like 'sparkle', or 'spark'. Pronounced with gusto it is onomatopoeic, like the sound of a flint striking on steel to make the spark that starts a fire, or a universe. G-nysh-T!

Lewisian gneiss is well named. Coming together in its boiling mix were ingredients for other rocks – granite, marble, mica, quartz. Heat and pressure brought about – slowly, so slowly – a metamorphosis. Lumps of those minerals were squeezed and ironed into bands so that Lewisian gneiss, when sunlight dances on its crystals, seems to let sparks fly.

And then perhaps as long ago as 3.5 billion years the freshly baked rock that would one day form the bedrock of much of north-west Scotland was pushed up towards the surface of the molten earth for the first time. Like a leviathan it rose, emerging first of all close to what we know as Antarctica. Its odyssey began then. On melted deeps, driven by eddies and currents, it drifted north at the speed of growing fingernails.

More of the Earth's crust became solid, forming what geologists call the lithosphere, which we may walk upon, which cradles oceans. The Lewisian gneiss was part of one colossal landmass after another – Columbia ... Rodinia ... Pangaea ... Gondwana. Always the drift north. Impossibly slow. Continent-sized rafts of rock came together – unstoppable forces; immovable objects – or were torn asunder. More rock was cooked in Hell's kitchen and served up, mixing with older, changing and being changed.

What would be North America was ripped apart from proto-Europe. The Mid Atlantic Ridge formed, the scar upon the wound. An ocean, oxygen and hydrogen, rushed into the space. By 60 million years ago the dry land that would be the British Isles was in more or less the right place. The part that would be England had been on an odyssey of its own. The coming together with what would be Scotland is marked by a scar that matches more or less the line of Hadrian's Wall.

Although the great rafts of rock coalesced with invisible, imperceptible slowness, there was violence in the union. Collisions lasting aeons drove mountain ranges up into the sky. One stretching from Scandinavia to North America was taller then than the Himalayas now.

The Lewisian gneiss was a victim too. While it takes its name from the largest of the Western Isles, and is there as the foundation of a swathe of Scotland's north-west, the torturing of the lithosphere saw to it that the same rock, torn ribbons of it cast far and wide, is there in Canada and Greenland.

Around 5,000 years ago – a brief span for rock that is 3.5 billion years old – farmers living in the west of the island of Lewis began paying attention to a ridge of land overlooking a sea loch. Signs are they had it for fields first of all. Early in the third millennium BC they began raising rows of stones on the ridge and then in a circle. Single rows pointed more or less south, east and west. A double row, called the avenue, pointed north. Viewed from above, as none of those farmers ever could, the whole thing has something of the look of a Celtic cross. Generations later a burial mound was built inside the circle, off to one side.

This is the site called the Callanish Standing Stones – the original Gaelic is Tursachan Calanais. It is older than Stonehenge and the Egyptian pyramids and, once built, its meaning mattered and so it was remembered for at least 2,000 years. That is how long it was in use, one way or another. By 800 BC the climate in the north had changed and there was more rain than ever before, a ceaseless damp. The truth of the stones was lost by then, the place neglected or misused by those who had forgotten what it ever had been. A blanket of peat began to grow (more slowness), enveloping the stones and much else. Callanish slept, its meaning muffled, until the late 1850s when Sir James Matheson, owner of Lewis and sometime governor of the Bank of England, had his workmen clear away 5 feet of turf to reveal the stones once more.

Archaeologist Patrick Ashmore excavated the site during the 1980s. The stones defy the efforts of scientists to make sense of them; no one can even count the tally, you know, no matter how one tries. Old explanations persist, reappearing like damp patches through fresh paint. They are giants turned to stone, some say, for refusing Christianity. Or they were an observatory for ancient astronomers, starry men who followed without optic glass 'the whirling ways of stars that pass' (as Yeats put it in his 'Song of the Happy Shepherd'). At best you might concede the arrangements of stones do seem to bear witness to cyclical movements of the moon. There are other specialists, scientists among them, who say any presumed alignments are only coincidence, like patterns made by joining dots into constellations in the night sky.

Ashmore has acknowledged the possibility that the stones' location might have helped the farmers predict an event called a 'lunar stand-still'. Every 18.6 years the moon skims low over hills to the south, creating an optical illusion. 'It seems to dance along them,' Ashmore wrote in *Calanais: The Standing Stones*. 'Like a great god visiting the Earth. Knowledge and prediction of this heavenly event gave earthly authority to those who watched the skies.'

Knowledgeable folk thereabouts say the farmers quarried the stones from a nearby ridge called Druim nan Eum. Its western edge bears the scars, and unused monoliths are scattered about. Leftovers. All around Callanish there are other ancient sites, made of more of the bedrock. Callanish is the jewel but its setting is fragmented. However they came by their building blocks, the farmers could not have known they were some of the oldest rocks on the face of the Earth. Whatever motivated them to form a cross, it was not Christ.

The oldest thing any of us will ever touch or hold in our hands will be made of rock. There is no avoiding the fact, and there must be comfort in it too. It is fitting that the farmers had that rock, that Lewisian gneiss so old, for the building of their first great works, works that lasted ever after.

In the twenty-first century we are moving away from the rock, from the earth. Our gaze is elsewhere, often to the detriment of where we actually live. Plans are afoot to move to Mars and beyond. No wonder we care less and less about home. More and more we are moving away from the flesh and bones of us as well. Christianity promised life everlasting – life beyond the body. Now technology is making the same promise. Transhumanists imagine uploading their consciousness to 'The Cloud' and then downloading themselves again into synthetic bodies. Life everlasting beyond the reach of death.

I already know the choice I would make should I be offered one. I choose here on Earth and flesh and bone, however limited and finite. Some of my certainty is founded on the rock, the same rock our ancestors turned to in the hope of understanding and making sense of what was going on around them. I turn back to the rock. It has been here the longest and in some form will always be here. Whether or not we have souls – some essence that prevails – the rock of the Earth has a pattern made of energy and matter that persists over time. Thrust up from the earth, ground and worn to dust that washes to the sea, for the wheel to turn again. My connection to the rock, my faith in the rock, is the only immortality I will ever need.

Stirling Cup and Rings
and the bones of the earth

To know fully even one field is a lifetime's
experience . . . it is depth that counts, not width.
A gap in a hedge, a smooth rock surfacing a narrow
lane, a view of a woody meadow, the stream at the
junction of four small fields – these are as much as
a man can fully experience.

– PATRICK KAVANAGH,
'The Parish and the Universe',
in *Collected Pruse*

THE GROUND THAT matters most to me is the few square miles around my house in Stirling. I could stay here for years on end. Were it not for the need to go and earn money, often far away, I would stay here indefinitely. It is only a few streets and green open spaces but it is more than enough to keep a person occupied with the business of understanding what is going on. It is much better than far away. I know this now. More recently I have felt the need to know every speck and leaf, but I will never know enough. I try to pay attention but I am missing things all the time.

Looming above my house is a wedge of dark quartz-dolerite with a castle on top of it. The rock is part of a geological formation called the Stirling Sill, magma that flowed hot within Earth's crust and then cooled and hardened. This happened some time between 250 million and 350 million years ago. When the glaciers ground their way south much later and for the last time, only thousands of years ago, the Stirling Sill would not budge. In the case of the wedge above my house, it formed a shield that protected softer rock beyond. Geologists call the shape a crag and tail – the crag being the quartz-dolerite doorstop and the sloping tail the softer stuff gathered behind. Something very similar made the rock for Edinburgh Castle and the slope called the Royal Mile.

The magma that made the Stirling Sill found its way among seams of coal, the stuff of summertimes laid down in the Carboniferous period over 300 million years ago. Miners found intrusive layers of the quartz-dolerite in the way of their shafts and tunnels. Sometimes the magma had been too close, too hot, and destroyed the coal; in other places it baked that stuff of ancient trees into anthracite which is the best coal of all. Hundreds of millions of years of Earth's adventure right here, beneath the playground of my son's school, the fields where we walk our dog. How could a person know enough about all of that? So much is out of sight anyway, buried and never to be known by anyone.

Hundreds of feet below the France-Switzerland border, near Geneva, lies a circular tunnel 17 miles around. This is the Large Hadron Collider, the best effort by thousands of scientists from more than a hundred countries to peek into the nature of reality by studying the tiniest things in the universe. The LHC is the biggest machine in the world. In it, scientists unleash beams and streams of particles, sub-atomic particles, the merest motes, on collision courses. On impact, close to the speed of light, these particles shatter into smaller pieces. By studying the aftermath of such collisions it is possible better to understand the forces that held those particles together in the first place. To know big it is necessary to know small. As the nineteenth-century British mathematician Augustus De Morgan once quipped:

> Big fleas have little fleas
> Upon their backs to bite 'em,
> And little fleas have lesser fleas,
> And so ad infinitum.

Even the littlest things, moving so fast, take a lot of stopping. Picture those emergency lanes alongside steep downhill stretches of roads. Drivers of juggernauts with failed brakes may steer their vehicles into those traps, where soft sands and gravels dissipate the awful momentum and bring them to a halt. The LHC has cylinders of dense graphite, 30 feet long and 4 feet in diameter, carefully placed at the ends of similar off-ramps. Beams of particles may be sent there, burying themselves deep, many feet deep, in order to stop.

Circles have been put to use for the longest time by human beings grasping after understanding. The LHC is the biggest and the newest effort. The physicists of the LHC have said that most of the universe, 95 per cent or more, is made of something they call dark matter, dark energy. They know it is there, everywhere in fact, and although they cannot see it they are looking for it. Some 2,600 years ago, a Chinese thinker called Lao-Tzu wrote a book called the *Tao Te Ching* in which he stated: 'There is a thing inherent and natural that existed before heaven and earth. Motionless and fathomless it stands alone and never changes. It pervades everywhere yet never becomes exhausted. It may be regarded as the mother of the universe.' If that is not a description of dark matter, dark energy, I do not know what is.

Tao is a circle. Our species notices circles. A single stem of grass, vibrating in the wind, makes a circle in the sand on a beach. The fern uncurls from a small circle, getting larger; a breaking wave is a circle collapsing upon itself. The sun is a disc, and the moon. Our ancestors noticed those lights, and others in the sky, following curling paths that drew circles around the Earth. The more observant among them, watching eclipses of the moon and sun, might have noticed that the Earth casts a circular shadow. Other perceptive, thoughtful types surely noticed the round of seasons – an invisible circle, but a circle just the same. A circle has no beginning and no end. It is the most efficient shape, the largest interior contained within the smallest perimeter. (Manhole covers are made round because a circle is the only shape that cannot fall down its own hole.)

The first farmers in the British Isles made circles of their own. Somehow they found the time for great works, the compulsion irresistible. Their first stone buildings, for the dead rather than the living, were buried inside circular mounds. Newgrange and Knowth in County Meath are dated to 3200 BC. Other circles were made to enclose holy ground – ditches cut into the bedrock, as at Brodgar and Stenness in Orkney; into chalk at Avebury, in Wiltshire. After circular ditches (called 'henges' by archaeologists, which is mostly unhelpful: whatever its roots – German, Norse – 'henge' refers to hanging and is inspired by the unique confection of Stonehenge where sarsen lintels seem to hang on their uprights) came circles of standing stones, and then circles within circles. Inside the circle of Newgrange, a stone-lined passage aligned on the place of sunrise on Midwinter's Day leads uphill to a circular chamber. The chamber sits 6 feet higher than the entrance and yet the architects designed a 'light box' over the entrance lintel and calculated the angles to ensure that a thin finger of light entered on that shortest day and rekindled the fire of life with the lightest touch.

'And down the long and silent street,' Oscar Wilde wrote, 'the dawn, with silver-sandalled feet, / Crept like a frightened girl . . .' In County Meath in Ireland, sun at dawn in midwinter is a jewel most rare, but on a lucky morning that light will travel the length of the passage (60 feet) and at its end illuminate, for all of seventeen minutes, a triskelion

13

carved into the face of a monolith. A triskelion is an evolution of the circle, three spirals made by one unbroken line: three ferns uncurling; three breaking waves – who can say? It is a shape associated with all manner of thoughts, including the Christian Trinity, but in its most ancient manifestations, as at Newgrange, is taken to suggest infinity, the ceaseless unspooling of time.

The obsession with circles was strong in these islands. There are more here than anywhere else. The oldest henges are on Orkney, but having caught on the fashion spread like measles the length and breadth of the archipelago until the whole place was infected with the spots.

Every day I walk our dog round a path that skirts a golf course. It was laid out in 1869, just seven holes at first; in 1892, legendary golf course maker Tom Morris added his touch. The course sits in part of what Stirling folk (known as Sons and Daughters of the Rock) call 'King's Park', acres set aside eight centuries ago when a park was open woodland where a king might hunt deer. This is the oldest of its sort in Scotland, named for Alexander III who fell from his horse at Kinghorn in Fife while riding home to his young wife. His only heir was his granddaughter, seven-year-old Margaret, the 'Maid of Norway'. She died on the journey to succeed him (of seasickness, some say) on Orkney where the oldest circles are, and so set Scotland on course for the Wars of Independence, William Wallace, Robert the Bruce, Bannockburn 1314 and all that.

From just beyond halfway round the outside of the course, on the way home, the best view is towards the rock and the castle. Beyond are the Ochil Hills, made of andesite and basalt – more works of earthly fire. Most conspicuous is the cowpat summit called Dumyat. This is a corruption of Dun Maeatea and remembers a fort ('dun') held by an Iron Age tribe that ruled before the Romans. History lies over Stirling thick as fog.

As well as the big view I try to take in the small, of which everything else is made, away from Dumyat and the castle on its rock, down towards my feet. A patch of bedrock exposed in the grass like a knee through torn trousers. Just yards from a fairway it is, nonetheless, most definitely in the rough, with tussocky grass and shrubby bushes all about, and a little copse of trees. The first time I noticed the rock was three years ago. The low light of early morning made plain, by the casting of shadows, two concentric circles etched into the glittering surface – sharp relief for ancient work, weather-worn. At the centre of the circles is a shallow dish, hollowed out. The whole is like fossilized ripples around the dimple from a dropped stone. It is a creation of farmers of the Neolithic – the new Stone Age, 4,000–6,000 years ago, give or take – and called, by archaeologists, a cup and ring. The cup mark is an inch or so wide, and a thumbnail deep – small, but no small effort in rock as hard as this. The first encircling ring is 6 inches across, the second more like 9. Usually the rings are part-filled by moss. Depending on the light, the shade, there are the seeming ghosts of other shapes on the rock, another cup maybe. They are too faint now to be sure.

Close by the cup and rings, not a minute's walk away, is a high point made of more exposed rock and affording all-round views that may have inspired the carving of the circles. According to the transactions of the Stirling Natural History Society for 1907 there was once a cairn nearby, a cist, long gone now but from which a funerary urn was taken and lodged in the local museum.

It is all layers hereabouts; mixed and folded geology made of history as well as rock. The jumbled bedclothes of time. The golf course is the topmost, the youngest. The outskirts of the town; the castle on its rock close by the Church of the Holy Rood where James VI and I was christened and John Knox preached fire and brimstone; the King's Park for the monarch's hunting; the lost fort of the Maeatea – all of it and all of them are squatters on the rock, Johnny-come-latelys. Long ago farmers paid attention to the rock, made a tomb of some of it for

Copt Howe
and the marks of the ancestors

... the greatest and the most original of the
spells ... we inherit from the earliest pioneers of
our race. It was the most imperative and the first
of our necessities. It is older than building and
than wells; before we were quite men we knew it,
for the animals still have it today; they seek their
food and their drinking places ... by known
tracks which they have made.

— HILAIRE BELLOC,
The Old Road

PHYSICISTS LIVE IN hope that one of them might write a theory
of everything – a few lines of maths to make sense of it all.

Long ago we all had songs for understanding the world and the best
way through it. They were passed down from one generation to another.
By singing those songs a person might find the way from place to place
and know how everything came to be and what it meant. Landmarks
were named in order so that there was no need to be lost. These songs
are forgotten, except in Australia where the Aborigines still cling by
fingertips to the edge of the elder world. We, however, are lost in

landscapes we do not properly remember, far less understand. The mountains and valleys, wide rivers running and lakes of deep water, caves of dark and cliffs sheer, ancient trees and white waterfalls all remain but without the songs we cannot know what we used to know. What we have instead are plain facts, sound bites snipped out of the timeline, a scientific understanding that separates everything into the smallest particles.

A retired nurse friend of mine says that if she could, she would bottle the benefits of a walk and administer it to all. In the developed countries we have evolved into a species that mostly sits. Even when we travel – especially when we travel, even over thousands of miles – we sit. This has come only lately to the human animal. Our ancestors stood on hind legs and started walking millions of years ago and kept right on going. Their pace gave them time to see everything, every step of the way. They felt the landscape with their feet, touched it with their hands, smelled and tasted it, and so were part of it.

Even the way we walk – striking down with the heel and rolling our weight forward on to the ball of the foot and then the toes – is the stuff of an ancient rhythm drummed on to the skin of the Earth. For some few thousands of years the rich had horses to ride, and which pulled carts that might be sat upon. Everyone else walked. Until mass transport arrived in this country towards the end of the nineteenth century, trains mostly, and then those who could afford to do so rode inside them.

The old ways are still there, not so easily erased, fading but still readable. The Lake District's Langdale Boulders sit where they have sat for uncounted thousands of years. On account of nearby steps over a drystone wall, some call their place Chapel Stile; others say Copt Howe. From a distance the pale grey boulders might be browsing elephants. Up close they are as big as houses, made of volcanic ash compacted and hardened ages ago by heat and pressure. Climbers practise by crawling like flies on the vertical faces. Less obvious are artworks etched and carved 5,000 years ago. Neolithic farmers took the time to scratch and peck all manner of marks – spirals, rings within rings, shallow cups, dots and geometric shapes. They are faint now, best seen in the shadows cast by the sun of an early morning. In style they are obvious kin to the cup and rings I walk my wolfhound beside in Stirling, their message as unknowable.

The Langdale Boulders mark the beginning of the way up into the fells that form the Great Langdale valley. On its northern side are the shattered peaks called the Langdale Pikes – Loft Crag, Pavey Ark, Harrison Stickle and Pike o'Stickle. During Neolithic times the latter two were destinations for farmers in search of material for axes. The tools they made, called by archaeologists Langdale axes, were coveted far and wide. A quarter of all the polished axes found so far in these islands hail from those two peaks. Geologists call the rock andesitic tuff, or greenstone. Like the stuff of the elephantine boulders it is, all of it, ancient ash made mud by rain, and rock by geology's patient processes. Langdale axes are sublime, lustrous as jade or deep water. It is hard to think they were ever wielded for felling trees – perhaps not only that: surely they were gloated over like jewels. Thin ribbons, veins of coloured marbling, the best of them are like strands of cirrus trailing over sky, or spikes of lightning. The veins are also fault lines, weaknesses that would have compromised their use for felling trees. Archaeologists have sought to understand why they were so wanted, if not for work, and have suggested it was the remote and precarious location of the raw material that made magnets of them – magnets for men. Those farmers had taken to burning rather than burying their dead – turning them into more ash, and smoke that rose. Since the smoke, made of the spirits of the dead, did not return to earth it may have seemed the sky was also heaven. The valley's topmost peaks were the last of the tribal land touched by those ghosts and so the rock was blessed, made holy.

The way on foot up into those heights is long and wearying. Some of the old quarries are on faces so exposed and precipitous they pose a threat to life now just as they surely did then. Any journey up into the fells in search of that prized and priceless stone might have been the stuff of quests for would-be heroes, a rite of passage for boys being made into men, maybe. We call the marks on the Langdale Boulders *art*, but only because they are abstract to us and meaningless. Just as likely they are words and phrases loud and clear in a language we can no longer read, far less speak. Or maybe they were maps, directions to the quarries or to heaven, even exhortations to those intent on the climb, words of prayers for the muttering by those venturing into the space of spirits. Something like 800 prehistoric 'art' works have been found in England – certainly no more than a fraction of all that were made. Often they are close by special places, by buried dead or over-looking grand views of the wide world. It is easy to think each of them marked a way, a track, an old road leading from somewhere to else-where . . . 'the great forgotten language, the lost lane-end into heaven, a stone, a leaf, an unfound door'.

Like the tracks made by sheep and other beasts, the ways our ances-tors knew and used were maintained by constant use, worn and cut into the landscape by footsteps alone. Those that led across the chalk lands of the south of England lasted longest – chalk being the best of all surfaces at retaining lines cut in this way. White lines worn into green hillsides, viewed from a distance, may have inspired other artists to make their horses and naked giants. And so, while ways on chalk might yet survive, others on softer soils less able to retain a shape or trailing over harder rock (that bore no trace bar the lightest patina made by soles) are long gone.

Ways and tracks were the first creations of our species because it mattered to life and limb to follow the best routes through the other-wise unknown. The writer Hilaire Belloc has pointed out that favoured ways lead walkers to river fords, to low saddles between high lands, beneath and beyond dangerous cliffs and other hazards to points and places where the going is safest and easiest. Those travellers who leave the ways and strike out on their own are often destined to waste time at best or, at worst, to face disaster. Worn and tested ways make sense and persist for good reasons. A person might do well to think long and hard before pioneering a new route through the morass or over mountaintops – just as any would-be revolutionary ought first to stop and think why he would break with the way that has worked. Old ways are venerable by right and deserving of respect.

In *The Old Road*, Belloc wrote about how it matters to study 'something of great age'. By so doing it was possible almost to re-inhabit the past time, 'not merely to satisfy a curiosity or to establish aimless truths: it is rather to fulfil a function whose appetite has always rendered History a necessity. By the recovery of the Past, stuff and being are added to us; our lives which, lived in the present only, are a film or surface, take on body – are lifted into one dimension more. The soul is fed. Reverence and knowledge and security and the love of a good land – all these are increased or given by the pursuit of this kind of learning.'

We say the world has grown small. From the warping windows of planes we have a God's-eye view of all that has diminished, that we have diminished. We criss-cross continents in hours and circumnavigate the whole of it in a day or two. But in the hills above the sharp-edged fields of grass tamed for our eating are the remains of the ways. Faded (and still fading) as any cup and ring mark on the Langdale Boulders, the dotted lines of the old ways are mostly overlooked. We would hardly let our children loose any more to play in places we have forgotten, or never even seen, and so those places go untouched by the generation that will succeed ours, hiding in plain sight. No one walks and so the ways, once worn deep, grow shallower and shallower. They are healing up after all this time, closing over like water does when we remove our hands from it.

Before the cups and rings are gone for good, before the last of the ways are smoothed out, we could make songs of some part of it, new songs to replace the old ones we have forgotten. It matters a great deal that we find our way back into the real world of the landscape. It matters to make again the old pilgrimages to the places that were special and sacred to our ancestors. Too many of us are strangers to our own land, washed up in towns and cities and shipwrecked there, surrounded by the ocean of the natural world. There is salve for the soul in the natural world and if we make time to walk there, remaking connections, our hearts will thank us. We could walk past ancient stones and remember, or wonder at least, why marks were made upon them by our kind.

2.

Family

Laetoli Footprints
– first family, family first

Men are men, but Man is a woman.

– G. K. CHESTERTON,
The Napoleon of Notting Hill

FROM TIME TO TIME, at Goldcliff on the coast of South Wales near Newport, archaeologists find ancient human footprints in the mud of the Severn Estuary – or Môr Hafren, as it is in Welsh. There is no predicting when they will appear; they are surprise presents every time. Now and again the retreating tide is in a generous mood and a few more are exposed. The feet that made the prints belonged to hunters of the Mesolithic, that middling swatch of the Stone Age that began when the glaciers withdrew after the last ice age 12,000 or so years ago.

People dependent upon the gathering of wild food were drawn to the sea in search of shellfish, seaweed and birds' eggs, as well as fish for netting and seals for spearing. The coast was a ribbon between two worlds – the land and the sea, the living and the dead. Vast mounds of emptied shells, amassed over many seasons, were repurposed as tombs for the ancestors, graves scooped out when needed and corpses interred within. The remains of food for the living swallowed the empty husks of the dead; life and death mixed together between worlds. Debts accrued and debts repaid, round and round and round.

Each time a clutch of footprints appears in the silty mud of Goldcliff there is a different glimpse to be had of the private past of people long ago. Like pages parted from the spine of a book, scattered and then happened upon one by one and out of order, each trail recounts a few phrases of a story. Sometimes they reveal the path taken by a lone adult. Always they are the prints of bare feet, toes splayed wide by a lifetime of freedom from any kind of shoe. The distance between the individual prints in a trail, the stride pattern, allows archaeologists to tell if the hunter was walking or running. At other times the waves withdraw and offer up the story, glazed and shining, of adults and children walking side by side. It is impossible not to have them holding hands in the mind's eye. Mothers and sons, fathers and daughters. Here and there are delicate trails left by deer, their hoof prints faint but flawless.

I saw some of the footprints for myself, just once. Archaeologist Martin Bell, from Reading University, let me join him and his team for a foray on to the dour grey sludge of the mudflats. He and they were on the estuary already when I sallied forth from the coast alone, following and sometimes clinging for dear life to upright wooden poles all in a line and gently rotting, marking the route. My feet in borrowed Wellingtons sank deep into or skited upon the glaur that clung and made halos like Flanders mud on Tommies' boots. I was aware of every print I made, looking back over my shoulder to see the glyphs recording the tale of my passing, though they would not last the day (or would they?). The sky was pewter flat and felt close enough to touch. There were indignant seabirds, and the mud I disturbed smelled over-ripe.

No amount of purple prose can match the sensation to be had on seeing a footprint made in mud thousands of years ago. How many times have you left a trail of your own upon a beach? How often have you walked absentminded and hand in hand with a loved one? Who would ever think the prints left behind might last millennia – not as fossils turned to stone but ephemeral as a cloud of breath exhaled on a wintry day and caught somehow for ever, just as it is? Imagine that was all the proof that you and yours ever existed. Without having to be told I could see for myself the impact of the heel striking down first, then the ball of the foot, then the toes. I put my hand into the glistening hollow of one and knew my skin was where his or hers had been. Everything we call history had happened in the years between their passing and my arrival but there we were together for an instant, hand and foot.

The preservation of such mementos is a fluke and happens at other places around our coasts. In the moments and minutes after the hunters' passing long ago, the tide rolled in and filled the prints with sediment. Each wave brought more, building layer on layer like laminate until the space so briefly loaned was reclaimed. Each tide repeated the motions of gentle burying. By chance, at Goldcliff, the ever-shifting course of the Severn moved itself away soon after, writhing snake-like day by day until the tide no longer came that way. The surface was submerged instead beneath other layers that formed, of peat and such. Thousands of years passed and the curved tadpole traces of life, left and right, yin and yang, were left suspended like shrimps in jelly. More recently, the Severn came again. Waves stripped the overburden until the prints, soft as the day they were made, were exposed, sensitive to the touch as skin beneath a fingernail.

Martin and his team had seen it all before, and while I watched and wondered, hunkered down and traced with my finger outlines left by ghosts, they set to with their cameras and drawing boards. The awful irony is that the prints' revealing is their unmaking, and for ever. Having waited thousands of years they return to the light for only a few hours, or even minutes. The suspended, weighted thread of time is rewound, the world exhales a held breath, and they are gone for good.

And so it is the mud of Goldcliff I think about when I read the story of footprints found in 1976 at Laetoli, to the south of Olduvai Gorge, in Tanzania, and excavated two years later by palaeoanthropologist Mary

Leakey.* Instead of estuarine mud, the prints Mary saw were made in volcanic ash. As well as human prints there were those of elephant and rhino, giraffe and buffalo, wild cat and wild dog and more, even the tiny impact craters of plump droplets of the rain that made a receptive mush of the ash, that gave it the power to remember. The seventy human footprints at Laetoli made a trail for 30 yards. Just like the Welsh ones far away, they show heel strike first, then ball of the foot, then toes. The strides are short, likely made by short legs. But while the prints I saw and touched were, Martin said, around 8,000 years old, the so-called Laetoli footprints were made 3.6 million years ago.

Mary Leakey's evidence settled what had long been a debate between experts in the field of early humankind. On one side had been those who said the move to walking upright on two feet had freed the hands for making and using tools – that it was walking with a straight back that set the course for civilization. Those on the left of politics have called it the labour theory of culture, as though it were gainful work that made useful citizens of us. On the other side were those who said walking came long before tool-making. Since the earliest tools we know about are only (only!) 2.6 million years old, it seems our ancestors were up on two feet at least a million years before any of them felt the need to sharpen an edge or knap a hand axe.

In his novel *Rituals*, Dutch journalist Cees Nooteboom wrote, 'Memory is like a dog that lies down where it pleases.' Earth has no memory, so far as we know, but the footprints at Goldcliff felt like memories just the same. Inside the rosy-pink meat of our brains we make moments permanent by flattening a trail through stands of synapses, like a path trampled through a field of tall grass. The more often we walk the same way, the more the memory is made fixed so that we might easily come that way again. Those prints I touched seemed like

---

* Along with so much of their vocabulary, even the specialisms of archaeologists have off-putting names as twisted and knobbly as the petrified spines of dinosaurs.

that to me, an otherwise random glimpse upon which the camera's shutter fell for the keeping. What might have been washed away, smothered out of existence soon after its making, had been transformed into something that lasted. Those hunters and their families in prehistoric South Wales would have had no reason to expect that their walk across the estuary might outlive them. The truth is that seeing those footsteps felt impolite, an intrusion, like a glimpse of something private.

For good or ill, with or without a memory, the Earth has kept some moments back. Since they have lasted it might be worth paying them attention.

Mary Leakey was not a product of any university. She was an illustrator when she met and married the more famous palaeoanthropologist Louis Leakey and began working alongside him (eventually, some say, leaving his efforts behind as she followed her own path). They were already separated when he died of a heart attack in 1972 (a fossil skull clutched in his hands), four years before the discovery of the footprints that made her famous, too.

Having studied the trail of prints in ancient ash she then learned to read their story. They were made by two adults and a child, a small family perhaps. The three kept close for a while and then one adult (Mary preferred to think it the female) took a few steps away from the others. In an article published in the April 1979 edition of *National Geographic* she wrote: 'At one point, and you need not be an expert tracker to discern this, she stops, pauses, turns to the left to glance at some possible threat or irregularity, and then continues to the north. This motion, so intensely human, transcends time. Three million six hundred thousand years ago, a remote ancestor – just as you or I – experienced a moment of doubt.'

Maybe all that time ago our ancestors were already bonded, tight as clumps of cells from which something complex might grow. They were small and slight, those first of the Australopithecines, our distant relatives; naked, without tools or weapons and vulnerable to the larger beasts that prowled. Frail or not, their long-fingered hands reached out towards the edge of cleverness. Our kind had almost everything to learn then. Ahead lay tool-making and farming, weapons and war, village life and city life, writing, flying and rockets to the moon. Even so, even then, it was seemingly in their nature to care about each other.

It was right for the one to put the others' needs ahead of her own. Either our kind knew it all along or they had learned it – learned the terrible lesson of the loss of valued others to the jaws and claws of beasts; learned to beat a path to a better sort of life. Maybe Mary was right and the mother of the child sensed something amiss and had to check, and felt relief when she had done right – when she found no threat at all and so put her mind at rest. Footprints on beaches, breaths exhaled, and yet at Laetoli, as at Goldcliff, we are invited to look again and then again at moments most fleeting. We have been safest in families for the longest time. We know this. Like the first family we know about, we must put family first.

Shanidar
and entertaining angels unaware

There was a crooked man,
and he walked a crooked mile.

— ANON. (ENGLISH NURSERY RHYME)

NOWADAYS THE PEOPLE of the west hold death at a distance, are horrified by the thought let alone the sights and smells of it. Dulling eyes, faces sliding into hollows beneath cheekbones; blueing lips and piebald bruising where stilled blood thickens; stale and sour exhalations from innards settling; rigor mortis. Take it away, hide it away and neither tell me nor show me. None of it is pretty, but all of it is real.

We hardly need look back as far as the Mesolithic for times when the corpse was welcome in the homes of the living and not readily surrendered. Only a hundred years ago it was deemed right, felt right, to sit around the bed – whole families and neighbours – to contemplate and talk about the newly deceased there among them with face washed, hair brushed and fingers clasped upon the bedclothes. While that hair and those nails added their final millimetres (news of the cessation of life having not yet reached those distant ends) there would be a grieving and a talking, a reminiscing, in the presence of the loved one. Not so very long ago death was another guest and space was made for him even in the marriage bed.

So it goes. At Les Eyzies in the Dordogne, in southern France, a pale lid of rock at the base of a cliff casts a shadow and so makes a shelter against sun and rain. It is called Abri de Cro-Magnon by the locals (*abri* and *cro* are both French words for a cave or rock shelter; Magnon was the owner of the land), and there, in 1868, more old bones were found. Excavated by geologist Louis Lartet, the remains added up, more or less, to four adults and a baby. Among the bones were familiar trinkets – shells with holes drilled through for stringing, a keepsake fashioned of tooth enamel or ivory of some sort, pieces of reindeer antler that had been worked and shaped by human hands for purposes we lack the wit to discern. The best of the adult skulls capped a cavity that made space for a large brain, large even by modern standards. The adult bones were gracile and yet showed signs of heavy wear. Modern analysis suggests injuries survived, hard lives lived for forty years or more (a long time in those days). Some specialists have looked over the bones and suggested those folk would have cut impressive and imposing figures. Their radiocarbon dating reveals they lived and died the best part of 30,000 years ago and yet were they to walk into a room today, a room filled with self-styled alpha males and females, each modern he and she would likely lower their gaze and turn away from them – from challengers whose muscles were made hard by hunting mammoths, whose confidence was wrought by staring down death on a daily, nightly basis. The Cro-Magnons, as original marques often are, might have been the best of us. Like others of their vintage they were in the habit of sending their dead on their way with jewellery and tools for lives to come.

All over the world it has been the same, and for the longest time. Far, far longer ago than the time of those layings to rest in the Dordogne other shadows of our sort (or as near to our sort as makes no difference) flitted over pale limestone walls in an ancient time of grief. In the Zagros mountains of Kurdistan in northern Iraq is a cave called Shanidar, its mouth a yawning, triangular blackness at the foot of a craggy blond spur. Used as a seasonal shelter by goatherds right up into the modern era, it has been home to humans of one variety or another for millennia. An American anthropologist called Ralph Solecki excavated the interior during the 1950s and 1960s and found all manner of evidence of occupation. Most famously his efforts unearthed the remains of as many as ten skeletons of *Homo neanderthalensis*, a version of humanity abroad upon the Earth from perhaps 400,000 to 25,000 years ago. First identified from remains found in the Neander Valley (*thal* means 'valley') near Düsseldorf in Germany in the 1850s, those ancestors of ours suffered some bad press early on. Heavy-set and with a tendency towards a prominent ridge of bone shadowing the eyes, the Neanderthals were first visualized as lumpen knuckle-draggers, little more than ape-men. More recently, given access to more remains of the same type, palaeontologists and other scientists have come to see these ancestors as closer to us in many ways. Red hair was commonplace among them. Proof that there was even interbreeding between them and *Homo sapiens* lies curled and sleeping in the twists of our own DNA.

A leap forward in our appreciation of these elder brothers and sisters was made possible, even unavoidable, by Solecki's revelations at Shanidar. One rickle of bones the anthropologists found they nicknamed Nandy, and it was plain he had endured a hard life made harder by physical handicap. His right arm was gone below the elbow, likely deliberately cut away; what remained above the site of primitive amputation suggested a birth defect that would have rendered the limb feeble anyway. His joints were riddled with arthritis and it seems unlikely he could ever have served his folk as a hunter like the other men. There was evidence of blindness in one eye, too. Nonetheless, crippled or not, half blind, he had lived into his forties, a ripe old age for a Neanderthal. His front teeth were worn and ground down to stumps in a way that suggested he had used them for gripping all manner of materials – a

33

clamp in lieu of a hand made absent. That he had lived as long as he did is surely testament to his having been valued by the troop of which he was a part. Perhaps he was clever in ways they valued, or had made of himself a reservoir of memory and wisdom. When he came to die his remains were buried beneath heaped earth and piled stones. In death he was not discarded or abandoned, put away at a distance, but, like those others exhumed nearby, kept close instead. Near Nandy's burial mound was evidence of hearths so Solecki supposed he might have been the tender of home fires and that those who missed him chose to plant him near the warmth that glowed after his time, but without casting his familiar broken shadow.

Close by the east wall of the cave were found the buried remains of another man. Like Nandy, he had lived into his forties – another elder. They had laid him down on his left side, curled like a baby in the womb. Palaeontologists winnowed the soil that had been the fill of his grave and found it dotted with pollen – daisies and white yarrow, dark blue grape-hyacinth and yellow St Barnaby's thistle, hollyhocks and woody horse tail, and more besides. Much of the pollen was only a scattering of individual grains but some was found in clumps and clusters, suggesting it had gone in upon him still cradled in the anthers of whole flowers freshly cut. Pragmatists have considered the leavening in the mix and concluded that that flowery dust insinuated its way into the grave long after the burial, burrowed in by small animals or tunnelled through by bees and other insects. Inescapable, though, is the thought his mourners laid him down in a bed they had first lined with fragrant matting and then covered him in blooms collected from the slopes surrounding the cave. Radiocarbon dates suggest that funeral scene was played out no fewer than 50,000 years ago.

Love is ancient and not only ours. It might be unwise to say much about bones that were ancient in the ground in a world so unimaginably strange. That said, it could be humbling to allow for the possibility that others have been better than us at cherishing the old and the crippled. Surely it matters to consider that love, loving care and grief might transcend us, that those emotions and responses are not exclusive to our kind. A species that came before us, that was a few hundred thousand years old before we arrived, was apparently careful with its folk in life and in death. Some palaeontologists doubt the Neanderthals had speech, believing they communicated in other, simpler ways. Readers of the Bible used to recite by heart that in the beginning was the word. But it is possible – surely it is possible – that love was there before the word. Our emotions are not new, but rather the legacy left by relatives who eked out lives in a world unimaginable.

Of all the loved bodies of Shanidar, for me it is Nandy's that carries the strongest latent charge. His few bones seem to pose question after question ... who, when, why? Of the many, the one I mostly dwell upon is what it was about him that they valued so, those kin of his. Theirs were hard lives in a wild world. Death would have been to them a commonplace, so too terrible injuries inflicted by the beasts they hunted and that hunted them. Nandy was likely incomplete from birth, with only one good arm. Later he lost an eye: a half-blind half-man. He must have been dependent on the effort and bravery of others – a hindrance and a drain on resources, some might say. And yet they kept him among them so long that arthritis set into his bones, and his teeth ground down to stumps.

The remains we find in the ground reveal some things – more and more as our science grows cleverer – but not why someone was of value. Individuals, as it turns out, might reveal themselves as priceless for all manner of reasons, and not all of them obvious. Even 50,000 years ago in a world of monsters, our ancestors had the wisdom to know there are infinite ways in which a person might prove invaluable. We should not be quick to judge. Maybe we should not judge at all. We would do better to be minded to care for each other just in case, 'for thereby some have entertained angels unawares'.

Çatalhöyük
and a harvest of children

A little later, remembering man's earthly origin,
'dust thou art and to dust thou shalt return,' they
liked to fancy themselves bubbles of earth. When
alone in the fields, with no one to see them, they
would hop, skip and jump, touching the ground
as lightly as possible and crying, 'We are
bubbles of earth! Bubbles of earth!'

— FLORA THOMPSON,
Lark Rise to Candleford

FOR MILLIONS OF years, all of nature's experiments with humans
gave birth to hunters and gatherers and scattered them thin across
an empty world. That way of life – the pursuit of wild animals, foraging
for wild harvests – is often portrayed as a lost idyll, the Garden of Eden.
Polymath writer Jared Diamond has even lamented the uptake of farming around 10,000 years ago. Those first farmers, he said, finding and
following a new way in a crescent of fertile land in what we know today
as Iran, Iraq and Syria, had more food but lesser lives. In Greece and
Turkey at the end of the time of ice, male hunters stood around 5 feet
9 inches tall; their women averaged 5 feet 5. Five thousand years later

men were typically 5 feet 3 inches tall, their wives around 5 feet. The daily grind of farming had ground them down. Fixed in place in their fields, gravity gained a better grip on them and pulled them to earth. Even now, modern Greeks and Turks have not regained the height of their hunter forebears. In *The Worst Mistake in the History of the Human Race*, Diamond described the adoption of agriculture as 'a catastrophe from which we have never recovered'.

The hunters hardly had it easy. Their rootless, restless lifestyle meant they had to limit their numbers, winnowing their own. A mother and father could carry just one toddler apiece as they kept up with the tribe. In a world without any obvious means of contraception, other than abstinence, infanticide must have been a fact of life. Until the younger children were perhaps four or five years old and able to trot alongside the rest, any other babies would have had their lives snuffed out at birth – likely a hand tight over the mouth, the nose pinched closed.

Farming was better for families. Settled life in a permanent home and a reliable food supply allowed for more offspring; more children meant more labourers, more land cleared, more fields worked, more food. Farming let mothers keep more babies.

For the first six months of life a baby believes she and her mother are the same thing. She has no concept of her individuality. Some time during the seventh month, or thereabouts, the awful penny drops. It is among the first and most fundamental realizations of life, the original game-changer. She starts crying any time her mother leaves her, even for a short while. She experiences separation anxiety. She has understood she is alone in the world. It is a permanent state, this understanding – the number one fact of life. Close family is insulation against the reality of being alone. It is not a cure, since there is no cure for reality, but it is the best help.

About 40 miles south-east of Konya, the seventh most populous city in Turkey, are the remains of a very old village. This is Çatalhöyük. An English archaeologist called James Mellaart found and partially excavated the place in the first half of the 1960s. Çatalhöyük is a *tell* – which is to say a manmade mound left behind by hundreds or even thousands of years of building on the same spot. First a few houses are built and occupied. As people's needs and moods change, those are demolished, the rubble levelled and new structures built on top. Repetition – year after year, generation after generation – sees the mound rise like a loaf in a warm oven. *Tell*, or *tel*, is a Hebrew word for a mound, and related etymologically to the Akkadian *tillu* which describes a mother's breast. The Farsi words for *tell* are *chogha* or *tepe*; the Turkish word is *höyük*. Whatever you call them, such sites are good news for archaeologists because all manner of revealing remains and artefacts are preserved there, trapped in and between the successive layers and telling the story in the right order. A *tell* like Çatalhöyük is a treasure chest, a thick palimpsest for people hunting clues about how our ancestors lived and furnished their lives.

Çatalhöyük tells a tale of families that wrapped themselves against a cold and lonely world 9,000 years ago by living together cheek by jowl, as jam-packed as bees in a hive.

Not far from Çatalhöyük is an even older village called Boncuklu Höyük. People there lived in oval-shaped houses arranged in a ring. It was inhabited around 10,000 years ago when the time of hunting and gathering in that part of the world was loosening its long hold on the lives of humans. Those villagers still hunted, and only gathered and processed wild-growing grasses that were the ancestors of wheat and barley. They were not farmers yet but something was happening to the way they understood how they might best make their way in the world.

Another English archaeologist, Ian Hodder, excavated Çatalhöyük in the 1990s. Before they tamed the wild grass, wrote Hodder, the people living in that part of Turkey had to tame their own wild natures. They had to make of themselves beasts of burden, sons and daughters of toil. Once that was done the one certain crop was more of us.

Psychologists have wondered if the first step in that process of change

38

was something happening inside the human brain, or at least the brains of some humans. I have wondered if the decision was not pushed by mothers tired of burying babies.

At the same time as they started farming – or maybe before – the people living on that south-western edge of the Anatolian Plateau sought solace in making shapes in clay, external expressions of internal thoughts. Heads of bulls, sheep and goats; fat female figurines with sagging breasts and drooping bellies distended by bearing and weaning young. Perhaps they worshipped mothers first of all, fertile women – and then imagined a fertile Mother Earth, bearer of unlimited food for unlimited babies.

Clay mattered so much to them they built their village beside the marshes that were its source. The fields they farmed were miles further off, a long walk away, but it was more important to those people to be close to the clay, the mixed spit and dust of the mother god from which all else might be moulded.

In the sweat of thy face shalt thou eat bread, till thou return into the ground; for out of it wast thou taken: for dust thou art, and unto dust shalt thou return. (Genesis 3:19)

They started building houses, homes for families, so close together there was no space between for streets or even alleyways. Mellaart made a plan of the houses he found and it looks like a clump of living cells that have divided and multiplied without separating one from another, like a living sponge or the tight gathering of energy in a star.

Since there were no streets to walk on, or even doors or windows to the outside, they settled for small square openings in the roofs that let folk in and smoke out. Each family must have come and gone by ladders and made their way from place to place across the rooftops. Yet there were no shared walls. Each house, though tight against its neighbours, was a distinct unit in and of itself, a determined cube. Walls and

39

roofs were made of timber and reeds, slathered with clay that was carefully smoothed as we might use plaster. Every year, or maybe as frequently as every month, more clay was applied to maintain the integrity of the structures. The houses were all alike, each with a square-shaped main room 20 feet to a side and linked to a smaller storage chamber. There were central hearths, ovens for baking, floors covered with reed matting, raised platforms for display, moulded alcoves for storage. Often the interiors were decorated with life-size heads of bulls made of clay, with real horns (they lived near a volcano with two cones that might once have had the look of a horned beast). Rather than leave the wild behind they brought its shapes and shadows into their homes. They were separating from the wild yet anxious for its presence.

It all seems so closely bound as to induce claustrophobia; a whole community of between 3,000 and 8,000 people held in one tight, almost suffocating embrace. The dead were kept close too – bodies curled like unborn babies wrapped tight with cords, chrysalids, and buried beneath the floors. Underneath a single house the remains of sixty-four individuals were found. All about the village their rubbish and waste was packed, human waste included, in a great stinking midden that insulated them even more in a collective, collected fug of humanity. They were hoarders, letting nothing go, not least their beloved dead.

Çatalhöyük was a living village for around 1,700 years, which is a long time – as long as the stretch from the birth of Jesus Christ to the Union of the English and Scottish Parliaments. If ever a house grew dilapidated, in need of replacement, the old one was carefully demolished until only a few feet of the outer walls remained standing. The cavity was filled with building rubble and a new house raised on the footprint.

They farmed wheat, peas and lentils and other crops besides. They kept sheep and goats and hunted wild cattle, deer and horse. From the nearby marshes they took water, fish and fowl. For storage they wove reeds into baskets and made some of the first pottery in the world from more of the clay, fired in their ovens. Obsidian – black glass from the fires of the Earth itself – was collected or traded from people living further north and made into polished mirrors. Flint was worked into blades, fitted with wooden handles carved in animal shapes.

They were the first of their kind, those infant farmers, almost a new species. What we know today – lives of rising with the sun and working until dark, the endless round of chores, our daily bread – was learned from their experiments with the clay and the emmer. Farming spread from them and others like them, a veritable virus, changing everyone and everything. It started with, and was all about, families.

Çatalhöyük means 'the mound at the fork in the way'. We cannot know what those farmers called their home, if anything. Their village is a glimpse of people at a fork in the road, thinking and feeling their way into an unknown future, understanding where they came from and aiming at a likely destination too. They were among the first to turn their backs on millions of years of hunting. The scattered hunters had been spread thin, but these farmers came together, concentrating their energy as nature dictates.

We have witnessed the inevitability of it all, the clumping and clustering of energy and matter, by looking far into the universe and watching stars and galaxies – bright, intense pinpricks in the emptiness. We can see the same by looking back at our ancestors, understanding those farmers were subject to the same irresistible law of nature, coming together close as could be.

At first they were alone in a world full of hunters, separated from the familiar and insulated against a new reality. Those families were some of the first in the world with many children, all young together – more energy. It was a seething, humming nest; a ball of cells dividing and dividing, fizzing with fertility. It was the family that gave birth to all the billions of us.

3.

House

Olduvai
and the oldest house in the world

Home is made for coming from . . .

— ALAN J. LERNER,
'Wand'rin' Star'

MY WORLD ORBITS our house, the centre of my universe. It is where my family lives now and where we might live always. We chose this house because there is space in it for our children and, if need be later, our children's children. We have imagined our possible future and decided it may be kept safe, held together by the gravity of the house that might contain it. In hope of persuading the future to be kind to us we make propitiatory sacrifices of effort and time, like pagans inside a circle of stones.

When I was a student at Glasgow University in the mid-1980s it was fashionable to imagine prehistory as a utopia, our ancestors wandering as Earth's children. Looking back on my lectures and lecturers now I can see the prism, made of politics, through which we were encouraged to view it all. The government of the day was of the right, our department of archaeology somewhat of the left. The message was implicit: before our ancestors were corrupted by the sickness of greed, there were millennia of egalitarian peace when hunters cooperated with one another and

45

women were valued as fellow providers; when people pooled resources and seldom quarrelled. There was an Eden. We were left to imagine all property was theft. I swallowed it whole. I overlooked the hook then, but I have felt it since.

House. Home. I look into my heart and wonder why I ever thought everyone – anyone – was happy to wander, rootless, for a lifetime. For every soul that is content to keep moving there must be another that wants only to stay put. The nomads are still among us, right enough. Herders of cattle and sheep criss-crossing the high latitudes; hunters in what remains of the forests and on the grasslands; travellers, gypsies and tinkers closer to home. By far the majority of us put down roots long ago and upheavals now, in the face of war or want, are hard to bear for those set adrift. The world's next wars will likely be fought for the space in which to settle down. Right now uncounted numbers are risking all in the hope of finding new, permanent homes. The desperation for a place to call home is acute.

Today the United Nations guesses one billion people – one in every seven souls – might be on the move. They are roaming within their own countries or across national boundaries. Surely almost every one of them wants to stop somewhere, and for ever. It is an old urge, ancient. A house. A home.

By the village of Howick, in Northumberland, archaeologists excavated the remains of a house built the best part of 10,000 years ago, at which point the familiar outline of the British Isles was still being drawn and re-drawn. It was a protracted process, spread out over thousands of years. During the last ice age so much water was locked in the glaciers that the sea was as much as 160 feet lower than now. What would become an archipelago was for a long time a peninsula of north-west Europe on to which people simply walked. The world warmed, the ice melted and the sea rose. Around 8,000 years ago the planet shrugged for a moment and an undersea earthquake off the coast of Norway sent a great wave across the North Sea. This 'Storegga Slide', as the geologists have called it, and its attendant tsunami made a broad brush-stroke. The line drawn cut our ties with the European continent and more or less defined the eastern and southern seaboard of the British Isles as we know it today. Those people resident beyond the reach of the great wave were all at once islanders.

It was an amateur archaeologist who found the Howick House, built when the bridge to the continent was still intact, having noticed flint tools that had tumbled like jewels out of a sandy cliff above the sea. A team from Newcastle University was summoned and soon it was clear there was more than just flaked stones. Around a shallow, circular hollow in the sand a frame of wooden stakes had once stood, all angled towards the centre in the manner of a tipi. The only physical proof was the shapes of holes left behind, dark circles in the paler sand, but they conjured an image of a structure built not for one night but to last life-times. Roofed and clad in whatever reeds and grasses were available in Northumberland 8,000 years before the birth of Christ, it would have been big enough inside to shelter an extended family. The floor was dotted with the remains of fires, a succession of them buried one upon another, telling a tale of many years of habitation. As well as providing heat and light they had been used for roasting hazelnuts, preserving food to help see the tenants through the winter months. Radiocarbon dates obtained from those hearths revealed the house was in use for a hundred years or more. It is impossible to be sure, but the evidence hinted at a permanent settlement used for generations. Rather than the notion of shadowy figures flitting ceaselessly across the landscape, travelling light, at Howick it seemed some hunters made themselves a home. Such a small thing to say, so normal to our way of thinking. But that some hunters chose to put down roots and live out lives that orbited a fixed base, coming and going from a place made special to them, alters our perception of that time, those folk.

Those shallow foundations in the sand are the foundations of all the settled lives lived in these islands since. The grand Georgian pile of

Howick Hall is nearby, a Grade II listed building that was home to Prime Minister Charles Grey, the 2nd Earl Grey – he of the tea that legend has it was mixed and perfected by a Chinese guest to suit the water that still flows in Howick Burn, water once drunk by those Mesolithic hunters.

The roots of home run deeper still, much deeper. In 1913, German palaeontologist Hans Reck was the first to find bones of ancient humankind in the Olduvai Gorge in Tanzania. The claim he made for the skeleton he found – that it was half a million years old – was dismissed by most as fantasy. Louis Leakey, that maverick in the fields of palaeoanthropology and archaeology, joined Reck in the valley in the 1930s and spent the rest of his career insisting the place was the cradle of humankind. His wife Mary, who would find the footprints at Laetoli, was there in the valley for many of the discoveries of what Louis called 'near-men'.

It was only in 1871 that Charles Darwin had published, in *The Descent of Man*, the notion that since chimpanzees, our closest living relatives, come from Africa, then the earliest 'true-men' and women likely had their origins there too. Science struggled with the thought for years and the Leakeys' subsequent claims for the great antiquity of the bones and tools they found in Olduvai were often met with ridicule. Some of what Louis claimed was debunked in his own lifetime, but his assertion that Africa cradled the first near-men and the first true-men is broadly accepted as scientific fact.

The images evoked by what we seem to know about our Adams and Eves are like glimpses from unquiet dreams. Anthropologist Henry Bunn, from Wisconsin University, has claimed that as long ago as two million years the near-men were picky about prey. While others imagined our earliest ancestors scavenging – waiting in line behind lions and hyenas and then sifting through the slavered leavings – Bunn found evidence that they were instead discerning diners. At a butchery site in Olduvai he found bones of antelope, gazelle and wildebeest left behind by human hunters from 1.8 million years ago. By studying teeth left in the jawbones of the slaughtered animals he could tell what age they were when they were killed. While lions and leopards brought down whatever they could – old, young, ailing, whatever – the human hunters had taken only adult animals in their prime. Bunn imagined them in ambush, crouched in the branches of trees, waiting until the right beast passed beneath. Dropping upon them from a height armed with spears, they could kill what they preferred.

It was in this way, by making high-protein meat a reliable staple, that they inadvertently grew bigger brains, not for themselves but for their descendants. While other primates settled for a mostly vegetarian diet, one that demanded long, energy-sapping guts, humans chose energy-giving meat from prime targets. From the seedling brain of *Homo erectus* – just 500 or 700 cubic centimetres – came larger and larger iterations until the time of *Homo sapiens* with three times the volume of the rose-pink meat that made possible everything else.

In 1931, Louis Leakey was joined for a season of excavation at Olduvai by fellow British palaeontologist Donald MacInnes. At a site Leakey called DK (D for Donald, K for *korongo*, the Swahili for 'gully') they found human remains, rough stone tools, animal bones and, close by, a circular setting of stones about 18 feet across. These were natural lumps of volcanic rock but had been placed by clever hands to form what Mary Leakey interpreted as the base of a shelter of the sort still made by modern peoples around the world. Upon the foundation of stones, a solid windbreak, might have been raised a lighter tent of branches roofed with whatever vegetation was to hand. A rose by any other name, it is a house, and it is 1.9 million years old – the oldest house in the world.

I do not suppose anyone would go so far as to suggest it was a permanent home but it looks and sounds a lot like a base. The best part of two million years ago it seems our ancestors, with potent little brains cradled beneath slight caps of bone, were thinking of staying put.

Perhaps their evolutionary path had brought them to a point where their babies and infants could no longer cling to their mothers for protracted periods, like the young of other primates. Since nursing females could not so easily accompany the males on hunting and gathering expeditions they needed to stay back at some pre-determined place of safety, a camp. At Olduvai we seem to see the first such effort, a place to wait and to ponder the chances of those abroad. Such a development implies a great deal. For one thing there is the suggestion of different roles for the sexes. For another it surely means that for the first time food was not eaten on the spot, as soon as it was found or taken. Instead it was carried back – carried home, to be shared with remembered others waiting there.

Here is the antiquity of forward planning, of picturing a future and taking steps to make it better for those who are cared about. There in the dust of Olduvai so very long ago are scratched the outlines of home and the family meal. The safety of family, inside a house, was not taken for granted then and should not be now. In a changing world we might at least understand the need of others of our kind to stop moving, to end the trek somewhere, and stay.

Skara Brae
and a stage set for drama

. . . a story about a world elsewhere, and a family
whose names many knew, whose house had been
large and populous with griefs and happinesses
that had once seemed endless . . .

— JOHN CROWLEY,
Little, Big

A S OFTEN AS I have visited Skara Brae and for all the clever pages
I have read about it, there is a stubborn part of me that cannot
help but think it a fake. *Of course* I know it truly is a Neolithic village,
5,000 years old: a perfect nest of houses, with flushing toilets and beds
of stone for sleeping and dressers of stone for making a show of special
things. So perfect is it though, so in keeping with what a person might
want of a Stone Age village, there is that lingering suspicion it is only a
film set.

Visitors are told the village was swallowed all at once and in antiquity
by a terrible storm. A scattering of beads was found in a doorway, they
say, a necklace torn from a woman's neck as she fled the waves and their
smothering burden of sand. Scotland's Pompeii, only with sand instead
of a pyroclastic flow of scorching ash to bury and stop time. Then forty

51

centuries of stony sleep until a Second Coming fit for description by Yeats; another storm, in 1850, and a rude awakening.

Some say nonsense to all the talk of revelation – that the find was no surprise at all to folk living by the southern part of the Bay of Skaill in the parish of Sandwick on western Orkney Mainland. They had always called the lumpy, grassy bump there Skerrabra and knew it for a buried Brigadoon.

Excavation after excavation took place, first by landowner William Watt alone and then with Orcadian antiquarian George Petrie. Other gropings by other fingers, sometimes out-and-out treasure-hunting looters. His Majesty's Commissioner of Works raised a seawall in 1924 to protect the ruins from further inundation, and three years after that came the first real archaeologist. He was Vere Gordon Childe, Australian by birth but professor of archaeology at Edinburgh University by then. Childe was a Marxist, preferred writing to digging, and in summertime wore shorts, and socks held up at the knee by suspenders. He favoured a long black macintosh, even over those shorts, and like Indiana Jones he wore a fedora hat. There endeth any similarity between fact and fiction.

Childe thought Skara Brae was Iron Age – an error uncorrected until radiocarbon dating in the 1970s, after his death – but his years of work put the place on the map. He was a giant of his discipline. His ideas came into and went out of fashion, sometimes tainted by accusations of racism, but he was first to use the c-word – *culture*. Having acquired the notion from anthropology he imagined cultures made of common traits – such as house styles, pottery forms, tools and burial rites – and roaming across the world with minds of their own. He also envisioned ways of life changing rapidly sometimes, under the influence of new ideas, new technologies. His commitment to Marxism, to communism, likely inspired his use of the word 'revolution' to have his readers think of sudden, dislocating change for the better.

Ironically there was ever something of the lost and homeless about

Childe himself. On 19 October 1957, back in Australia, Childe dropped to his death from a 1,000-foot cliff in the Blue Mountains called Govett's Leap. By some accounts he had laid aside his personal effects before stepping from terra firma, making it seem like suicide. Others noted he had left his bill unpaid at the hotel where he had been staying: a man as ferociously tidy in his affairs as Childe, they said, would have left no such loose end if he had truly made a rendezvous with death. In a letter he sent to a friend – asking that it not be opened until ten years after his death, whenever that occurred – he wrote that 'life ends best when one is happy and strong'. Perhaps at sixty-five he felt old age on his shoulder and the senility he dreaded above all. Perhaps he knew his time was past, that the world of the future belonged to others of a different sort, a different culture. House and home are elusive sometimes and for some, so too peace of mind. Having once left Australia, and despite searching high and low for answers to it all, it seems Childe never found his way home again; never found peace, short of the drop.

A revolution is what Childe had called the change from nomadic hunting to settled farming, and so it was – the Neolithic Revolution, the greatest upheaval our species has known. After 200 millennia of following the wild herds, and the promise of ripening wild foods, we settled down and made ourselves at home. At dawn we rose to clear fields, plant fields, weed fields, protect fields, harvest fields. Others stayed behind at home to bend backs not over earth but over quern stones for the grinding of seeds into flour – the daily grind that has been our stone-faced mistress. We became watchers of the sky – for clouds that meant rain for sowing, sun that meant ripening and drying of crops. We kept our necks craned, looking up to track the moon and the seasons.

After millennia of feeling owned by the land our settling down made owners of us all. We owned the land and owed it to ourselves to change it, modify it, to remake it in our image. It was the start of territories, walls and wars. We built circles of stone to match the cycling of the years and of life itself. We built houses of stone for our beloved dead, the ancestors whose mouldering bones were proof of our claims on the land (this field is mine because it was my father's, and his father's before him, and they live still inside that tomb). We built houses for ourselves to live in for lifetimes and then pass on to our children.

Home. The word itself sounds like a moan of heartfelt longing, and so a house, a home in which to live for ever, is a perfect answer to ancient questions: where do I belong . . . where may I lower my defences and be me?

At Skara Brae the way from visitors' centre to village is past signs saying the settlement is older than Egypt's pyramids, but nothing prepares a person for their first sight of the place. In recent years there has been a fondness for the Danish notion of *hygge* and its connotations of cosiness. In Scots there is *courie*, which means to snuggle close somewhere warm and safe. Skara Brae seems home to both. Those farmers dug their houses into a great midden, a rubbish heap, then packed more malodorous mass about and in between, for insulation. These were people who knew and held the corpses of their dead and handled their sticky, stinking bones. They spilled the guts of fish, animals and birds and worked their skins and furs, staining their fingers with gore. They lived in windowless, one-roomed homes, whole families wreathed in smoke from fires and wrapped in the always-unwashed funk of togetherness. Their tolerance (even appreciation) of the world of smells was different from our own. Homes packed around and topped with rotting leavings, steaming warm in winter storms, must only have been welcoming.

It was the sea that laid bare Skara Brae, and the waves are ever present, biding their time and ready to consume more. The illusion created is of seafront property, but 5,000 years ago the beach was many miles away. Trees are scarce on Orkney now and would have been then, the lot having been swiftly cleared for fields and first buildings. For a while there was speculation the farmers might have watched the waves for timber swept from North American coasts and washed up on their shores. Now that we know the sea was nowhere near, such a suggestion seems unlikelier than ever. Whatever they roofed their houses with, or burned on the hearths in the hearts of their homes, it was not wood.

There may once have been more houses, taken long ago by ancient storms, but there are eight dwellings now, all connected by alleys and covered ways. Doorways are crawl spaces, the stuff of hands and knees. The guardians of the place keep one house pristine, behind a locked door and beneath a modern roof. Inside, archaeologists found all sorts of wonders; a landlocked *Mary Celeste* that seemed abandoned in a hurry. Beneath the stone bed they found the skeletons of two women side by side. Those ladies surely lived and died there, and when their lives were spent their family could not bear to see them go and kept them close as could be – so redolent of love and of disregard for any fear of death and the dead. This is some of what home meant.

Skara Brae may have been inhabited for 600 years. For all the colourful talk of an apocalyptic storm, precious things torn and lost in the flight before the waves, archaeologists have found no evidence of it. More likely the place was abandoned for other reasons, stretched over time. Years ago I visited another Orkney Isle, Swona. Just one and a half miles long by half a mile wide it might be a carelessly tossed turf, a clod washed away by the sea, but it was home to some. Its last inhabitants, the Rosies, abandoned their farm in 1974 and went to live and die elsewhere. Their cattle are resident, yet feral now in memory of the aurochs of old. I walked into the Rosies' old house and found it furnished still; a wireless radio on the mantel, a newspaper folded on the table and reading glasses laid beside, legs up like a desiccated locust dead on its back. Life on Swona had grown too hard and its people ebbed away like a tide, without drama of any sort. Still it felt furtive and wrong to be there without consent. I left the place as I had found it.

The houses of Skara Brae feel just the same. Once made, a home takes on its owners' presence like a perfume. If they are the last tenants and none replaces them, their time lingers after they are gone. Homes, houses make us move and act in ways so familiar we do not have to think. They are stages, and we as actors know our marks, our entrances and our exits. Farming, along with that Neolithic Revolution, made everything different, and for ever. Houses mattered most of all and every one was the same as every other. In 200,000 years nothing we have made means more than home.

The Great Pyramid
and the sterility of living in death

There is a law written in the darkest of the Books
of Life, and it is this: If you look at a thing nine
hundred and ninety-nine times, you are perfectly
safe; if you look at it the thousandth time, you are
in frightful danger of seeing it for the first time.

— G. K. CHESTERTON,
The Napoleon of Notting Hill

THE HEART OF Neolithic Orkney is the name given by UNESCO
to a group of Stone Age monuments on that archipelago's Mainland. Something began on Orkney 5,000 years ago. Avebury ...
Stonehenge ... Durrington Walls – those and so many other sites elsewhere took their best inspiration from Orkney. The Heart of Neolithic
Orkney was a source of infectious wisdom.

The UNESCO name is apt. Sometimes it feels like the heart of the
world. A person might sense they are at the centre of a vortex, of a spinning universe. And yet, and yet ... there is at the Heart of Neolithic
Orkney a sense of an idea not fully realized, an idea still hatching.
Stand in a house at Skara Brae and look at the stone settings – stones
for beds, stones for a hearth, even a dresser of stone for the showing of

precious things. Stand in the chamber of Maeshowe and look around the burial tomb's walls, up at the roof. There is ingenuity and craft, skill with stone. Walls raised at the Ness of Brodgar are better than any that would be built on Orkney for another 5,000 years. But drystone walls are drystone walls; there is only so much that can be said of them. Of course there would have been other materials – woven fabrics, animal skins and furs – to soften the edges. But all of it is rough-hewn. The standing stones of Stenness and Brodgar are undressed, unshaped splinters cracked from the bedrock and set on end. The rough edges, though, are part of the power to enthral.

The monuments at the Heart are the start of something; the white-hot spark of inspiration, older than Egyptian pyramids and Greek temples. The idea would be finessed elsewhere in other times but it is older on Orkney. If that first marque of our kind, Cro-Magnon, was the best of us, were the Stones of Stenness perfect at the first attempt? Maybe the polishing that took place later on and elsewhere with metal tools and marble was only gilding the lily. I don't know enough to say for sure. I do know that when I walk from stone to stone at Stenness or stand under the corbelled roof of Maeshowe, the understanding of the place is as out of reach as the sense of a dream on waking. Roughed out in Maeshowe and the buildings of the Ness is a striving after something more and better than was possible there and then. The builders knew what they wanted and aimed at that target as best they could in that time and place, isolated by geography and with limited numbers of people to do the work. For a thousand years they tried, sometimes levelling what had been built before and raising anew. Any time I think I am close to the meaning of it all – a glimpse in my peripheral vision – it slips past like a stranger in a crowd. The world has forgotten whatever was meant on Orkney at that time.

That forgetting is also for the best. That the idea was left unfinished and set aside after a thousand years of trying was in everybody's interests. Rather than dream endlessly among their stones, a changing world demanded new ideas of those farmers and they were forced to change tack. On Orkney, people moved on from that stony pondering – or rather they were moved on by events. The wind blew colder, the climate changed for the worse, life got harder and the great buildings became too much bother. The wind blew sand over the fields, over the houses. Crops failed and beasts died. Communities moved and fragmented. People found new ways to live – not crowded by the neighbours as at Skara Brae but in scattered farmsteads instead. They sought new answers to whatever questions they had. The frigid wind that blew was an awakening slap across the face, jolting them out of a trance. A thousand years of questing had been more than enough and now those farmers were cast out of their soporific Eden. The challenges they faced and met set them on course for the changes that were the making of them, the making of the future. Today there is no greater tourist attraction on Orkney than Skara Brae, a place of the living. It stands among the rest of the evidence of the time of the first farmers – the tombs and circles – testament to a living world that was never overwhelmed by that of the dead.

Far from Orkney, far away to the south and east in the territory once called the Levant (on account of the rising sun), life was always different. In Mesopotamia, or Sumer as it was known, rivers flooded the land and winds had blown from the beginning of time. Farmers found islands of high, dry ground and built their villages there. Working together, they cut channels for all the water and so made fertile fields. They won harvests in the face of elements they understood as fickle, vengeful gods. Any success demanded cooperation en masse. It was there in that world of threat of sudden floods that people realized a liveable world had to be won from chaos by their own efforts. There was no protection against the gods, no place safe enough under the sky, and in Sumer there grew a religion of pessimism and fatalism.

Ancient Egypt was another world governed by the flood – the annual flooding of the Nile. Hunting was giving way to farming in the valley there around 7,000 years ago. The people made copper tools and navigated the river in boats made of papyrus. To early architecture they gifted the column, being the first to make such things by bundling reeds together and covering them in mud that hardened in the sun. The fluting on later stone columns is a tribute to those first caked stalks.

By the fourth millennium BC there were two kingdoms in Egypt – a Lower in the north and an Upper in the south, each with its own king. While Sumerian society evolved from villages into cities and city-states, something different happened in Egypt. Within the kingdoms, people lived in small, simple villages. A few cult-centres developed – communities of priests serving a temple that the villagers visited from time to time in order to make their devotions. Towards the end of the fourth millennium, Menes, king of the Upper Kingdom, conquered Lower Egypt. At a stroke, Egypt became a unified entity, snaking 600 miles either side of the river that flooded every year bringing fertility to the land. The population continued to live in villages, and in time there grew at Memphis a great royal centre. At other times, in other centuries and at the whim of other great men, the focus of the kingdom would be up-river, further south at Thebes. Ruling over all – not as a man but as a god – was Pharaoh. Initially the word had referred to the land's ruling court; only later did it come to mean the man. Egypt had not known the stepping stones of cities, and important men ruling them. Instead there had sprung spontaneously the centralizing concept of absolute kingship.

During the Fourth Dynasty of the Old Kingdom, in the middle of the third millennium BC, the great pyramids were built at Giza. Greatest of them all – the ultimate house of the dead and the oldest and only survivor of the Seven Wonders of the Ancient World – was that of Pharaoh Khufu, or Cheops as the Greeks would later know him (and it). The build took twenty years and demanded the labour of thousands at any one time, to move into place more than two million blocks of stone weighing tons apiece. Each of its four sides measured 750 feet in length, completed with a margin of error of less than 1 per cent. The whole of it stood, in its finished form, more than 480 feet high and covered 13 acres. For centuries its very existence has fascinated, confused and beguiled the world's scientists and fantasists. Until the completion of Lincoln Cathedral in the early 1300s, with its wooden spire 525 feet high that blew down in a storm in 1548, the Great Pyramid was the tallest manmade structure on Earth. Its construction demanded coordinated effort by a well-fed, well-organized and motivated work force equipped with only the most basic of mathematics. Inside and beneath the pyramid's massive bulk are three chambers – one subterranean, a second near the centre called the Queen's Chamber and a third above called the King's. An empty granite sarcophagus was found in the King's Chamber. If there ever was anything of value in any of those spaces, it was looted long ago.

Khufu was king of what Egyptologists call the Old Kingdom. A Middle and a Younger Kingdom followed, spread across the best part of 3,000 years and separated one from the other by two so-called Intermediate periods during which invaders held sway. The inescapable achievement and triumph of Ancient Egypt was its longevity. In spite of the vast span of time, in spite of the kingdom being invaded by outsiders not once but twice, the Great Pyramid endured. A people who lived simple farming lives, sustained by the annual inundation of the Nile which brought fertile silt (a gift from Pharaoh), remembered who they were generation after generation.

At heart, though, they were a people preoccupied by dying. Whatever life might hold, from richest to poorest they dreamt most devotedly about what might come next, after life. Ancient Egypt gave little to the future that was not dead, or of the dead. The hieroglyphs were part of the progress towards representing sounds rather than things. For the longest time in Egypt the word *was* the thing, with no concept of any separation between the two. Object and meaning were one. Before the end they had begun to accept the concept that words are only identifiers for things, but even in this they likely copied from the nearby Sumerians. Egyptian art established a style and form that remained consistent for 2,000 years but that was again borrowed from the neighbours. Egypt, like the pyramids that everyone knows about, was one giant gravestone.

On Orkney in the time of the Neolithic, one generation of farmers after another had known a world of repeating patterns. The climate was kind to the crops and animals for the longest time. The lights in the sky were in perpetual, predictable, comforting motion. In the space between sowing and harvest, folk planned and built and demolished and built again. But after the climate changed and everything was altered, they were jolted on to a new path.

In Egypt there was no such correction and century after century the old pattern repeated, without interruption. The river flooded, the crops grew, the sun shone and the harvests were collected and set aside. Manpower was marshalled on a staggering scale, organized by a bureaucracy of unsurpassed attention to detail – only to raise the largest gravestones in the world. Men and women lived their lives, it seems, only in preparation for their dying. While the houses of the dead were made of eternal stone, the homes of those who bent their backs to the labour were always and only of mud brick that would be washed away and forgotten. No one cares to seek them out now, those places where the builders lived out their lives. Visitors to Ancient Egypt are come only to a graveyard, a home of the dead. In the battle between life and death in Egypt, death won. The Nile, bringer of life, was a rut – lush and fertile, but a rut. It was altogether a sterile and moribund way of living.

How lucky for Orkney and Orcadians, then, that circumstances beyond their control made them wake up, concentrate their efforts on the land of life. Alongside the tombs of their ancestors there are preserved the houses of the living, so that both sides of the story of a people might be glimpsed – yin and yang, alpha and omega. Life grew hard on Orkney, harder than it had been, but it was about living. The future held innovation – bronze tools and then iron and all the rest. New people came – Celts, Romans, Vikings. It was all new blood. So it was for all of the British Isles. Ancient Egypt made itself a backwater, a rockpool left behind and stagnating after the tide withdrew, never to return. Change is good. New is good. Ancient Egypt lasted unchanged and unchanging for 3,000 years. After those sterile millennia focused on death, the old girl died right enough, and for ever. Back in the Heart of Neolithic Orkney, all is rough, unfinished, a work-in-progress to the end. Unfinished – like life.

Choose a work-in-progress, a house as yet unfinished, however rough around the edges. Choose life and the living.

4.

Tenants

Dmanisi Skulls
– early tenants of this rented world

I shall not be there.
I shall rise and pass.

– STEPHEN VINCENT BENÉT,
'American Names'

D
URING THE FIRST two years of my degree at Glasgow University I studied medieval history. Of all the characters I read about, none lodged in my memory more firmly than Timur the Lame, the last great Mongol khan. To the Elizabethan playwright Christopher Marlowe he was Tamburlaine the Great, to Edgar Allan Poe and William Shakespeare, Tamerlane. There are multiple versions of his name and endless claims regarding his conquests and cruelty. He claimed he was fathered by a shaft of light that fell upon his mother as she lay sleeping. He called himself the Scourge of God and built an empire greater than Alexander's. He saw to the slaughtering of hundreds of thousands if not millions. He made 120 towers of heads severed from 100,000 citizens of Baghdad. The Ottoman Sultan Bayezid I – Bayezid the Thunderbolt, they called him – made the mistake of proclaiming himself mightiest in the world, and word of the boast reached Timur. He brought the sultan and his thousands to battle at Ankara, in Turkey,

in 1402 and utterly crushed them. Some accounts have Bayezid taken prisoner and kept in a cage that was dragged behind Timur's dogs for twenty years. He spared Europe – ignored it rather – because he regarded it as worthless and home only to barbarians.

Here in western Europe, many of us might be tempted to think we have always mattered in the world. We mattered in the end, of course, in the last few hundred years over the course of which our sort changed everything for everyone. But it is useful to remember there were ages when all the action took place elsewhere. While civilizations rose and fell between the Tigris and the Euphrates of Mesopotamia, and on the banks of the Nile in Egypt, our lot counted not at all.

A footnote in Timur's story has him lay waste to a town called Dmanisi, in Georgia. He may have had no designs on London or Paris or Rome, but it mattered to that khan to stamp his footprint into the dust of the Caucasus, just as those feet had traipsed across mud made of volcanic ash at Laetoli three and a half million years before. Dmanisi had history by that time, a great deal of it. Before Timur brought his blurring of Islam and shamanism (his banner bore a flying horsetail beneath a crescent), there had been Orthodox Christians for 800 years and more. Even they and their cathedral squatted on older times – traces of the Bronze Age at least. Sat at the crossroads between western Asia and eastern Europe, Dmanisi's inhabitants had watched everything and everyone pass by. The town grew rich, almost into a city, and its name was known for hundreds of miles around. Before Timur's horde came calling there were Seljuks and, after them, Turkomen. By the eighteenth century however the place was a lagoon, or a rockpool or an oxbow lake, left behind at last. The final wave had broken and shrugged away.

Palaeontologists began finding early human remains at Dmanisi, south-west of the Georgian capital Tbilisi, in 1991. There is an armful now, enough to clutter the surface of a kitchen table. A few rough stone tools were discovered too, pebbles clattered against other pebbles until sharp edges appeared on some. They all belong to the species *Homo erectus* that walked out of Africa during the time geologists call the Pleistocene, or the Ice Ages, which began 2.5 million years ago.

Look into the eye sockets of the five skulls of Dmanisi in hope of recognition, a family resemblance if you will. All have strange faces and each one is subtly different from those of its companions. Long faces – prognathic, as the scientists call them – sloping backwards from chin to brow, steep as a ski jump. Cavernous mouths packed out with big teeth. They are an elderly man, two adult men, a young woman and a youngster of indeterminate sex. The largest and most complete skull, that of one of the males, was found in 1995. Large in terms of its overall mass, it made room for the smallest brain of the five, just 550 cubic centimetres compared to the average *Homo sapiens* brain case holding nearly three times that volume. We cannot know what thoughts filled those cavities, how those like them comprehended all they saw. Surely no speech, no art created, but clinging to that elder world with fingertips flattened and whorled like our own.

Animal bones found nearby show those ancients shared their version of the world with sabre-toothed cats, giant cheetahs and other predatory frights. The *Homo erectus* remains were unearthed in what appeared to be animal dens, dark vaults into which their corpses had been dragged for rending, tearing and eating.

Palaeontologists say the five devourings were spread at intervals across a few hundred years, all of it happening around 1.9 million years ago. Nearly two million years ago . . . think of that! The discovery of those five, each with a different face like the variations you might find in any group of people, caused a commotion in scientific circles. Whenever a *Homo erectus* skull had come to light back in Africa, and was compared to those already found, the slightest variation between one and others was deemed to indicate a different species altogether. In this way the specialists had conjured a cast of characters – *Homo ergaster*, *Homo gautengensis*, *Homo habilis*, *Homo rudolfensis* . . . But the varied and various Dmanisi skulls, all but cheek by jowl with one another and with lives lived close in time, raised the possibility that, varied or not, they were all of one sort, the same sort, all crouched beneath the shelter of one name: *Homo erectus*, the upright man.

These upright men and women were abroad in southern Africa by 2.4 million years ago. This is deep time, the dark ocean beneath, and all but out of mind for our species. The first of them are closer in that near-eternity to the fleeting shadows of *Australopithecus* – those diminutive 'African apes' that are also our relatives – than they are to us.*

As far as we can tell, *Australopithecus* was the first to walk upright on legs that were like a man's and not like an ape's. But he and she were not human yet, not *Homo*, not quite. They could run though, over long distances while carrying loads in their arms, in that way apes cannot.

Homo erectus, their bones present in the hollow places beneath Dmanisi in Georgia, was of a species that shared the world and breathed the same air as little *Australopithecus*. This is more amazing to me than any story of Adam and Eve. Adam is from the Hebrew *adamah*, which is the ground – specifically the flesh-pink clay. It was

---

* Such voids in time are hard to take. *Tyrannosaurus rex* is closer to us than he is to *Stegosaurus*; we are closer to Cleopatra than she is to the Ancient Egyptians who built the pyramids. In the years after the Second World War, French historian Fernand Braudel, of the Annales School, developed the idea of the *longue durée*, the long term. If time is an ocean, wrote Braudel, then all that we human beings can perceive are the merest bubbles and foam on its surface. Those flecks and specks, coming and going in moments, are the years of our lives. The bubbles and foam are vexed by little waves, no more than cat's paws, that are the risings and fallings of empires. But down in the dark, miles down and far beyond the reach of any light at all, are the imperceptible flexings of deep time. We sense nothing whatsoever of those movements drawn out over aeons and they in turn lie upon the rock and sediment of the world. There, beneath all, is inertia – that languid tendency for nothing to happen, nothing at all.

from such stuff that Adam was made, and after the fall it was his fate to till the same clay from dawn until dusk, before eventually returning to it. The root of 'human', and therefore *Homo*, is the proto-Indo-European *dhghomon*, meaning 'earthly being'. We are human. *Homo erectus* is human too in a way that palaeontologists insist *Australopithecus* is not (the southern ape is denied the *Homo* epithet). And yet they shared space and time. Men and not quite men, human and not quite human. And there in Dmanisi lie the skulls of one of those species, the upright man.

For long archaeologists had them as ape-men, boorish dullards. More recently they have been accorded more respect, reimagined by some as thinkers, solvers of problems. In any event they travelled far and wide in the old world. After hundreds of thousands of years, *Homo erectus* spread north as far as the territory we know as Ethiopia. Some of them looked across the Gulf of Aden, likely at the narrowest point, from the spot we call Djibouti, and may have made their way over the water and on to the Arabian Peninsula. There were periods during the Pleistocene when sea levels were low enough to have allowed some simply to keep walking, over dry land. From Arabia they spread again, slow as dampness up a wall, until their sort were all over. That path laid down two million years ago – *the selfsame route* – is still being followed by migrants and refugees on the move out of Africa today. It is the way – The Way – and it is old beyond the reach of anything but imagination.

This world – these places we inhabit, give names to, fight and die for, exclude others from – is rented accommodation only. To me it is beyond fascinating that people lay claims of unyielding ownership upon their various patches in the way that they do. It is like flies arguing about who owns the horse they are bothering. Our species, *Homo sapiens*, is not the owner of this Earth, any more than was *Homo erectus* or *Australopithecus*. We are tenants and no more, with no title deeds. Beneath the floorboards of these rented rooms of ours are foundations

Lake Toba Eruption
– latest in a long line of near misses for humanity

For want of a nail . . .

— PROVERB

THERE IS A Gary Larson cartoon of a Stone Age classroom in a cave. A slab-faced Neanderthal teacher clad in a leopard skin stands at the front, addressing the pupils. All but one of his charges look just like him. At one desk slumps a glaikit creature, a much more primitive, knuckle-dragging monkey-man. Not looking at anyone in particular, the teacher says, 'I've got your grades here, though I'm afraid not all of you are moving up.'

The monkey-man is going to be left behind, and soon. This is evolution seen through the eyes of comic genius. The last laugh, a hollow laugh, comes from knowing what the future holds for those Neanderthals as well. They might think themselves safe from further pruning by the ultimate gardener but we know their time is coming too. Only the strong survive, and all the pinheaded monkey-men who could not cut it are history.

Like every other species, the various iterations of humankind have

73

been subject to editing. From rough draft to magnum opus, every word has been scrutinized by an unforgiving eye, and many cuts made. Every trace we have of all nature's previous experiments – *Australopithecus* (the knuckle-dragger in the cartoon), *Homo erectus*, *Homo antecessor*, *Homo heidelbergensis*, *Homo neanderthalensis* – all of it could be collected into a few crates. And those are the ones we know about, the ones whose fossil traces we have stumbled upon. Other marques, other versions of humanity – Quasimodo (by which Victor Hugo meant the rough approximation of a man) – have surely come and gone without leaving behind so much as a tooth as proof of life. Over 90 per cent of all the living things that have existed on Earth, plant or animal, are extinct. For all the dizzying profusion of life on Earth, Mother Nature travels light. All manner of her offspring drowned at birth. Others lasted hundreds of thousands, even millions, of years and must have seemed like chosen ones, but were still shown the door before the end. Mother Nature is a serial killer. This is neither a good thing nor a bad thing.

This home planet is 4.5 billion years old in a universe that is three times that age. *Homo sapiens* is 200,000 years old, a vanishing spark in cosmic time. There are seven billion of us alive today – far, far more at once than at any time in our history. It took until 1800 before there were a billion of us together for the first time. Whatever we are doing, right or wrong, it is speeding up. It is worth remembering we have at times clung to the ledge of existence, dangling above the void while Mother Nature stamped on our fingertips.

It seems several species that contributed to the eventual genesis of our own were, in modern parlance, critically endangered for periods lasting at least hundreds of thousands of years. For the longest time, our ancestors were worryingly thin on the ground. In a study of the genomes of two modern people, published in 2010, scientists at the University of Utah, in Salt Lake City revealed they had identified tiny packets of very old DNA left over from ancient ancestors. Dotted among the modern DNA were occasional short stretches of code that geneticists call Alu (*Arthrobacter luteus*) sequences. Those are stub-born survivors, best above all at making copies of themselves that occur again and again in the same genome, like the same phrase repeated over and over in a long book. Once inserted into a genome, Alu sequences are seldom lost or removed and so often evade nature's editing process. They cling on, being passed down from the stuff of our ancestors to the stuff of modern humans. When a geneticist finds an Alu sequence in the genome of a modern person, it is like an archaeolo-gist finding an ancient hand axe in the foundations of a modern house – it is proof of connection to the distant past.

The Salt Lake City geneticists had not one but two complete modern genomes to compare with one another. Whenever they found an Alu sequence in one, they looked for mutations close by. By comparing the various mutations in the two genomes they were able to estimate how much genetic diversity had been present in the DNA of those distant ancestors. The number of differences between the two genomes made it possible to estimate the size of the ancient populations of the ancestral species.

The science is mind-bendingly complex for general readers, but the results are nothing less than poignant: for millions of years, individual members of ancient species of a human sort were pitifully few in num-ber. *Homo erectus*, *Homo ergaster*, some of those that flitted like shadows through worlds and times unimaginably different from our own, were sprinkled only lightly through the Middle East, Asia and Europe: having had their genesis in Africa, some of their number had ventured elsewhere.

Working up actual numbers from the results of analysis of strands of DNA is difficult. Pushed to come up with something solid, those university scientists suggested each of the relict species might have numbered no more than 30,000 souls. Given that only between a half and two thirds of those might have been capable of breeding at any one time, the fate of a species might have depended upon just 18,000

75

individuals. And consider the realities of a breeding population of 18,000 spread from one side of a continent to another – Romeo in Spain and Juliet in Turkey.

The results are still being mulled over, set in context. Debate about what they truly tell us is ongoing. Since evidence of proto-humankind has been found all over Africa and Eurasia, there had previously been an assumption our ancestors were numerous and we were only being vouchsafed tiny glimpses of whole populations, in the form of fossils. That in fact those who provided the threads – which were eventually woven, with others, into the tapestry of *Homo sapiens* – had amounted to a presence best described as patchy for perhaps *millions* of years should be enough to make us quiver.

More harrowing still, we may at other times – more recent times – have been closer yet to the door marked EXIT. This we know because of discoveries in Lake Toba. Cupped in the caldera of a super-volcano in Sumatra, Indonesia, and measuring 60 miles long by 20 miles wide and 1,660 feet deep, it is the largest volcanic lake in the world. In 2017, biologists working in the rainforest south of the lake identified a brand-new species of orangutan. Orangutan is Malay for 'the person from the forest' and they are our closest relatives, along with chimpanzees, bonobos and gorillas.

The fossil evidence is slight, but it suggests that around 15 million years ago there was a fork in the evolutionary road. At that time there existed a species that probably lived in trees and weighed maybe 40lb. Some of them took the fork that led to chimpanzees, bonobos, gorillas and orangutans; the other stepped out on the road that led to hominids, us. As recently as 2001, biologists realized there were two species of orangutans, specifically the Bornean and the Sumatran. The new discovery in 2017 is a third, dubbed Tapanuli after the area of forest they inhabit. These Tapanuli orangutans might remind us of the predicament of our own ancient ancestors. As far as the biologists can tell, there are no more than 800 Tapanuli orangutans spread across a territory measuring just shy of 400 square miles. Their vulnerability to oblivion is like that of our ancestors, just on a much smaller scale and happening before our eyes in the modern world.

Lake Toba was also the scene of the largest volcanic eruption in at least the last 100,000 years. The lake fills the crater left behind by the cataclysmic explosion. Vast, sky-filling quantities of dust and ash were thrown into the upper atmosphere where winds and the planet's rotation spread them into a darkening cloak. Archaeologists, paleontologists, biologists, botanists, climatologists, geneticists and others have debated the impact of Toba for a long time. Having risen into the atmosphere and hung suspended there for years, the dust eventually fell to earth and sea. It has been spotted, like a criminal's fingerprints, in cores extracted from the bed of the Indian Ocean, the Arabian Sea and the South China Sea; it has been identified from a depth of over 8,000 feet in a core from the Greenland ice cap and in another from Antarctica. During archaeological excavations in India, the same dust was found juxtaposed with layers featuring stone tools made either by Neanderthals or *Homo sapiens*. Suffice to say, that dust got around.

Disagreement persists, however, over whether or not the Toba eruption wrought widespread devastation. Pollen in cores from Lake Malawi dated to the time of Toba seemed to contradict any notion of a winter during which nothing grew. Archaeologists from Cambridge University examined those Indian stone tools, unearthed at Jwalapuram in Andhra Pradesh from layers both below and above (and so before and after) the fall of dust and ash. Since the style and quality of the tools remained consistent, the team concluded the same population had persisted unperturbed in the area in spite of the eruption. Whether that population was Neanderthal or *Homo sapiens* is unclear.

Some scientists, though, allow for the possibility of enough dust in the sky to have caused a winter lasting ten years or more, spreading across whole continents. They imagine plant life withering and dying for want of life-giving sunlight, herbivores starving and human beings following suit. The most apocalyptic readings of the evidence have the human population cut back to just a few thousand individuals, eking out an existence in corners where sunlight poked through the dust cloud, giving life a fighting chance. Whether caused by Toba or not, temperatures around the world, which had already been dipping downwards for tens of thousands of years, appear to have gone into an even steeper decline around the same time. It is a tantalizing coincidence.

Among other things, geneticists seek to understand why we are so varied in appearance despite our shared, and recent, African origin: skins white, sallow and black; eyes blue, brown, green and hazel; Vikings and Zulus, San Bushmen and Mongols. For as long as a species has a plentiful supply of individuals, occasional mutations born to mothers here and there have little chance of breaking through, far less altering the nature of the majority. In a large and healthy population, such random occurrences are smoothed out of existence, disappearing like occasional droplets of colour into an ocean of clear water. Some geneticists allow for the possibility that a winnowing of the species, such as may have followed the Toba event, created what they call a bottleneck. A decade-long volcanic winter may have triggered centuries of glacial climate deterioration that in turn put many species under almost intolerable pressure. If the human population numbers collapsed and suitable mates were few and far between, mutations may have gained a foothold. Beggars can't be choosers, so to speak. If Toba truly was a near-Armageddon, then some of the variations on the theme of *Homo sapiens* may have slipped through then.

Some mutations are for the greater good. Albinism, which makes pale skin instead of dark, was advantageous to *Homo sapiens*. White skin requires far less exposure to sunlight than black skin in order to process Vitamin D from food – minutes a day instead of hours. Black skin, made dark by melanin, is best at protecting a person from potential damage caused by exposure to the strongest sunlight, nearest the equator. Pale people and their offspring have more chance of remaining healthy in gloomier climes north and south by avoiding the enervating and sometimes fatal condition rickets, caused by Vitamin D deficiency. The successful spread of the species, to the top and bottom of the world, would not have been possible without that single mutation.

Mother Nature does not care if we live or die. The book of life has been savagely edited, and the process is unstoppable. After millions of years of holding on to existence by our fingernails, we have had two centuries of exceedingly fruitful multiplication. But we remain vulnerable to mindless natural processes, known and unknown. Like Larson's Neanderthals, we might make the mistake of thinking Mother Nature stopped her experiment with humanity when we came along. Hardly: we are still being tested. Not everyone will make the grade – and likely through no fault of their own. Those least able to defend themselves will suffer most. As that teacher might have said, 'Not all of *us* are moving up.'

Lepenski Vir
and the salt of the earth

The woods decay, the woods decay and fall,
The vapours weep their burthen to the ground,
Man comes and tills the field and lies beneath,
And after many a summer dies the swan.

— ALFRED, LORD TENNYSON,
'Tithonus'

A LL AROUND THE world there are stories of the first of us being
moulded by God or gods from the stuff of the earth. In different
places different ancestors came to the same conclusion. It made sense
to imagine having been made of the soil and clay of the place.

When I walk my wolfhound around Stirling I know when she
detects the scent called petrichor because I smell it too. It is the coming
of rain. Leaves turn silvered backs to the rising wind. Gracie lifts her
head high, nostrils flaring. She breathes in deeply and snorts and
shakes her head, and the air excites her.

Petrichor – from the Greek *petros* for stone and *ichor* for the blood
of the gods – is the odour that rises from earth made wet again after a
dry spell. In the normal run of things, dead organic material is attended

to by actinobacteria in the soil. Much like fungi, they break down fallen leaves and plants into simple chemical compounds that will eventually be drawn upon for life by other living things. If there is a dry spell, a drought, the processes of decomposition slow and then grind to a halt. When rain finally comes – actually just before the downpour, when the air itself becomes damp and moistens the soil just enough – the work is restarted. A by-product of the breaking down of organic material is a natural alcohol called geosmin. This combined with other plant oils also occurring in the soil makes petrichor the perfume, or maybe the sweat, of the Earth (and earth).

Because we depend, as animals, on water for life, we are especially sensitive after a drought to the imminent onset of rain. All alcohols have strong smells but the very nature of geosmin, its precise mix, means humans can detect just a few parts of it per trillion molecules of air.

This is how and why we say we can smell rain. Rain itself smells of nothing of course, but the scent it raises from the earth, in an aerosol form that travels on the wind, enlivens us like a charge of electricity. In these indoor, urbanized times we pay less attention to the living world, or are encouraged to see it only as a source of things we can use, draw upon like a bank account we have not paid into. We might call this separation a progress of sorts, part of rising above the dumb animals. That we can still smell the coming of rain and be pleased by it is a reminder we are as sensitive to the condition of the earth as we ever were.

The Djerdap Gorge, on the border between Romania and Serbia, was cut out by the Danube River. Where it is orientated south-east, towards its middle reach, the river flows fast and deep. There spun whirlpools of great force, and their constant birling made sculptures of the rocks. The sun shines mostly on the right bank of the Danube at that point, and on a gently sloping horseshoe-shaped terrace kept secret by trees and cliffs, people made themselves at home 9,000 years ago. They were hunters and fishers, and the village they made where the gorge is narrowest is known to archaeologists as Lepenski Vir, which is the Serbian for 'red clay whirlpool'.

Pollen excavated from the lowest levels of Lepenski Vir – the time of the first human settlement there – reveals that birch trees and tsuga conifers grew nearby. This suggests cold temperatures in the past, a tougher climate than today. But down by the river, protected from biting winds by thick woodland and steep cliffs, people found a kindly spot and stayed. There was game in the forest behind them, fish in the river before them, and for miles around all manner of wild harvests for the gathering. As well as birch and conifers, there was beech, hackberry, juniper and oak for building, hanging creepers for binding and tying.

Opposite the sheltered shelf, on the far side of the river, is the looming presence of the peak called Treskavac, a vertical slab of pale cliff 2,000 feet high and standing watch over all. It is trapezoidal in shape (a triangle with its top cut off), which seems to have affected the thinking of the villagers at a fundamental level. From the beginning they built homes with trapezoidal floor plans, each shaped like a slice of cake minus the pointy end. Maybe taking their cue from the ever-present sentinel, its face in sunshine or in shadow, they raised a crescent of homes facing always towards the river and the rock. From the slopes nearby they gathered pink limestone marl. This they baked in fires and then ground to a powder which they mixed with water and ash. The result was a sort of lime mortar they poured and spread to form smooth, hard floors. It was as though the earth, this Earth, had told them what they might do and they had listened and heard and understood.

The houses of Lepenski Vir followed a pattern, a blueprint. A central rectangular hearth down the long axis of each house, timbers packed tight in their holes with stones – all of it set into the pink concrete before it hardened. A long roof pole slanted downwards from the high front of each house towards the low rear, supported by other uprights slanted in from the sides of the trapezoidal floor plan. The result was houses with wide, tall fronts that sloped down to low back walls. The back end of each roof pole was fixed to the bedrock.

Once arrived at – by whichever architect among the first of them – the design was repeated over and over for 2,000 years. Houses were built, scores at a time, lived in and then demolished and replaced with newer versions. Inside many were strange fish-men sculptures carved from large sandstone cobbles collected from the river. Wide eyes and gaping, gasping maws like landed fish. Some have interpreted them as representations of river gods. Archaeologists who have studied Lepenski Vir have debated whether the very first structures, with their careful floors and ever-watchful sculptures, were shrines. Maybe the people raised homes for their gods before they made any for themselves.

The villagers of Lepenski Vir were in the habit of burying their dead in a cemetery nearby. From time to time a few of the dead, adults and children, were buried beneath the floors of the houses, beneath the foundation stones of walls – intact skeletons or just skulls and jaw-bones. Elsewhere in the village a grave was found, the skeleton within laid on its back but with legs folded almost into the lotus position until it conformed (by accident or by design) to the recurring trapezoidal shape.

Those hunter-fishers of 9,000 years ago were the descendants of migrants out of Africa. As far as we know, outside of Africa all people are connected to those that walked out of that vast continent as long ago as 80,000 years. Within a few tens of thousands of years, part of that movement had passed through the Middle East and reached Europe. The latest DNA analysis – a science that day by day is cracking wider the window into our past – reveals those pioneers may have had dark skin and pale eyes.

Archaeologists and palaeontologists have long pondered the consequences of encounters between Neanderthals and *Homo sapiens*. The DNA of modern Europeans tells a story of couplings. While no modern African people have Neanderthal DNA in their flesh and bones, all

Europeans have as much as 4 per cent. Within a few thousand years of that contact the Neanderthals were gone, made extinct, but their echo is in our genomes. It may be that that resounding coming together, like flint on steel, made the spark that ignited all else. Something new, other, was stirred into the mix and we were made brighter, greater than the sum of the parts. It was in the aftermath of those unions that limitless creativity was conjured – spoken language for the first time maybe, tool-making finessed to heartbreaking perfection, some of the finest art we have ever managed. The path to the moon and stars might have begun with the first offspring of Neanderthal and *sapiens*.

There are varying estimates as to how long the Neanderthals clung on to Europe after our lot arrived, but by the end of the last ice age the vestiges had been wiped away like chalk dust from a blackboard. *Homo sapiens* had the rented accommodation all to himself.

However they survived the millennia of cold – and some experts have concluded it was a close-run thing, with just a few thousand individuals eking out an existence in southernmost Europe – by perhaps 12,000 years ago the ice was in final retreat and the human survivors pushed north again, little by little, generation by generation. Those that settled at Lepenski Vir were descendants of that movement back into the space on loan from the ice, maybe dark of skin and pale of eye. They knew they were made of the earth and floored their homes with more of the same. Every one of their houses faced the river and the sentinel; analysis of their bones reveals their diet was mostly fish from the river. They understood the world by sensing they were part of it. When they smelled the petrichor they knew rain was on its way.

The hunter-fishers lived like that at Lepenski Vir for two millennia – the same length of time Christianity has lasted in the west. It might have seemed to them that the way they had things would be the way things always would be. However long their tenure, though, they were only tenants like the rest of us. Far away to the south-east, in the territory of Anatolia, in Çatalhöyük and Boncuklu and other places like them, there were already villagers of a different sort. Analysis of their DNA suggests they were pale-skinned and dark-eyed – the opposite of the hunter-fishers. They had domesticated the wild grasses, emmer and einkorn – or been domesticated *by* them, made into farmers. The time of hunting and fishing was coming to an end and would be swept aside by the farmers.

This is the way of things, the way of people.

5.

Memory

Henbury Station
and meteorites and memory

Toto, I've a feeling we're not in Kansas any more.

— DOROTHY,

in *The Wizard of Oz*

TODAY IN SILICON Valley, California, technology visionaries look far ahead into the future. People like Peter Thiel of PayPal and Elon Musk of SpaceX are the new Moses and John the Baptist. These are the men behind research bodies such as the Singularity University and the Future of Humanity Institute, think tanks dedicating time and vast sums of money to imagining and then taking the next steps in evolution. Their endeavours are not the stuff of abstract theories, they are even now being made real in technologies close to the production line. For the prophets of the next age, the future is post-human.

Transhumanism is a way of thinking that is already decades old. In 1990, in an essay entitled 'Transhumanism: Toward a Futurist Philosophy', a forward thinker called Max More could define it thus: 'a class of philosophies of life that seek the continuation and acceleration of the evolution of intelligent life beyond its currently human form and human limitations by means of science and technology, guided by life-promoting principles and values'. Soon, they say, we will upload our consciousnesses (our souls?) to the digital universe, where they will exist as long as there is power flowing to the servers. Then there will be synthetic human forms – robots, cyborgs – into which a consciousness might be downloaded, so as to interact directly once more with the physical world. It all sounds exciting or hellish, depending on your point of view.

At the time when it was new to the world, the USP of Christianity was the promise of eternal life for every man, woman and child. It was a revolutionary concept. Where it had previously been a prospect at all, it was the preserve of the few – pharaohs, the bravest warriors and so on. Then out of the east came the notion that, in the eyes of the Christian God, all souls weighed the same. Commoner or king, it mattered not: believe in the One God and access to heaven was a dead cert.

Slow and steady scientific progress during the past few hundred years has all but done away with this notion. The nineteenth-century German philosopher Friedrich Nietzsche is usually credited with signing the death certificate of the Christian God in *The Gay Science*. 'God is dead. God remains dead. And we have killed him,' he wrote. His sentiments are usually taken out of context so that many folk now assume Nietzsche was celebrating the loss. In fact he was warning fellow travellers of his present, and of the future to come, that there would be a reckoning for the crime, and consequences; that the vacuum created by God's absence would pull in something else: 'How shall we comfort ourselves, the murderers of all murderers? What was the holiest and mightiest of all that the world has yet owned has bled to death under our knives: who will wipe this blood off us? Must we ourselves not become gods simply to appear worthy of it?'

The sacred game of transhumanism has revitalized the old hope of transcendence. Transhumanism being grounded in science, there is no talk of souls. Instead there is a 'pattern' – consciousness, or personal identity – conceived and understood as the product of biological processes. In *How to Create a Mind: The Secret of Human Thought Revealed*, futurist and transhumanist Raymond Kurzweil described identity as 'a pattern of matter and energy that persists over time'. So far, the pattern has been software running on physical hardware – the human brain and nervous system. Those wear out and die; however, the pattern – call it the soul, consciousness, identity – with the help of emergent technology might be made eternal, put beyond the reach of the corruption of any flesh.

In the end it comes down to memory; finding ways to remember and to be remembered for ever. If our always degrading flesh and bone cannot be relied upon to remember us, to keep safe for ever the pattern of us, then we might seek artificial means instead.

The Henbury Crater Field lies 80 miles south of the town of Alice Springs, in Australia's Northern Territory. According to scientific analysis, the cluster of craters there was made around 5,000 years ago by a nickel-iron meteoroid that broke up in Earth's atmosphere before smashing into a spot near the centre of Australia. It is estimated that our species has been abroad on that continent for as long as 60,000 years. It follows, therefore, that some of our sort may have witnessed the event.

By the latter part of the nineteenth century, Australians of European descent existed on what was known as Henbury Station, a property occupying several thousand square miles. In 1899 Walter Parke, one of its owners, wrote to an ethnologist called Francis Gillen to report his discovery, out in the vastness, of what he took to be man-made circular features. No further action was taken at that time and all went quiet until 1916, when a mineral prospector called James Mitchell came across a lump of nickel-rich iron in a blacksmith's shop in a town further south. When told it came originally from Henbury Station, he made plans to go there, finally doing so in 1921, when he found more of the same. Mitchell became the first documented white man to know the site for what it was: a set of craters caused by a meteorite. He said later that his Aboriginal guide, a local, had refused to get within a mile of the place, claiming it was taboo on account of being the site where a fire devil had come from the sky long ago and killed everything for miles around. News of all this was slow to travel – apparently on account of Mitchell being tardy in his reporting. In any event it was not until the early 1930s that he sent a sample of the metal to the University of Adelaide and the Henbury Crater Field came properly to the attention of the modern world. Scientists visiting the site would often hear from local indigenous people that the place had been visited long ago by a spirit from the sky that brought fire and death. Anyone drinking water from the place risked being 'filled up with iron'.

Debate has bubbled ever since. On one side are those who accept the meteorite strike was witnessed by people 5,000 years ago, who then described it to their children; in this way the story survived down through the millennia. On the other side are sceptics who say the event was forgotten long ago, that scientists brought the truth when they arrived to investigate the site. Only then did the 'fire devil' story enter the folklore. We cannot know either way.

A total of twenty-six meteorite impact sites have been identified in Australia. Of those, perhaps a handful happened during the 60,000 years of *Homo sapiens'* tenancy of the continent. It is no longer possible to discern whether stories that sound like fossilized accounts of ancient cosmic events are genuine witness statements passed down for thousands of years, or borrowings from recent incomers. Like a crime scene disturbed, the evidence may have been contaminated to the point where it is no longer admissible.

Fallible or not, memory is what makes us human. It is a collateral product of consciousness. Science says the universe is 14 billion years old (though that number keeps changing, flickering before our eyes like the aurora borealis). *Homo sapiens* is around 200,000 years old – a fraction of that unimaginable desert of time. As far as we know we are the only animals to have known consciousness. Without consciousness there is no awareness of self; without consciousness there is no awareness of time. We are the only animals to have *known* we are animals, and that time existed before we did. Since nothing was awake before us to take account of all those billions of years, then they might as well never have happened. Time started with us and all the years before our arrival therefore passed in no time at all. When our species awoke to consciousness, the universe awoke too, and for the first time.

Aboriginal Australians talk about all manner of events they claim happened long ago. As well as fire devils from the sky, they recount descriptions of droughts that lasted years, lifetimes. The clans of the interior remember a vast inland sea. Some of the traditional accounts marry up with the findings of modern science and geology; some do not. Traditionally minded Aboriginal Australians insist their people have always and only been in Australia. Palaeontologists, geneticists, biologists and others say different.

The dominant theory of the twenty-first century has the species *Homo sapiens* appear first and only in Africa. At some uncertain time, a portion of them began moving out of the great continent, through the Middle East and then into Asia and Europe, finally reaching the Americas via a land bridge across what is now the Bering Strait, around 25,000 years ago. Perhaps as long as 60,000 years ago the ancestors of today's indigenous Australians made the crossing to that continent from somewhere in southern Asia. But no folklore describes that odyssey, an epic journey lasting tens of thousands of years. Surely this is more interesting than wondering whether any one clan remembers a meteorite striking the Earth a few thousand years ago? It seems to me that that journey, out of Africa and onwards, was undertaken before our species woke up to consciousness. It seems to me that what indigenous Australians call the Dreaming is literally that – a time beyond the reach of memory, when to all intents and purposes *Homo sapiens* was still asleep in the manner of every species of life that had gone before. The very notion of a Dreamtime might imply that the descendants of the first inhabitants of Australia carry, like a half-remembered dream, an awareness of the time before the advent of consciousness. Their lineage might be so long, some threads of it still unbroken, that they remember the time before remembering.

We are a long way from Kansas, and no mistake. Every day, faster and faster, we are travelling further and further from the meat of us, the animal of us, the human of us. After billions of years of all life made of carbon, we have in our telescopic sights a life of machines. I do not say this is necessarily a bad thing; I only wonder if it might be important to notice the final step before we take it.

'Eeny, meeny, miney, mo' as one, two, three, four is all that survives of a counting system that was in the British Isles before the Romans. All over the north of England are relics of other systems. In Niddersdale in the Yorkshire Dales there are those who remember when shepherds there had yain, tain, eddero, peddero, pitts, tayter, layter, overo, covero, dix instead of one to ten. Fragments and fossils, broken away from their bedrock but still there. Careful, deliberate remembering is how we know ourselves as individuals, as members of families. When the memory goes, so too does the person. However much we surrender to the silica and the machine, we might do well to keep some remembering inside our heads. Fallible or not, it has been what makes us, us.

Coldrum Stones
and a space for the few

For the growing good of the world is partly
dependent on unhistoric acts; and that things are
not so ill with you and me as they might have been
is half owing to the number who lived faithfully a
hidden life and rest in unvisited tombs.

— GEORGE ELIOT,
Middlemarch

I N 2017 I visited the island of Rousay, off Orkney Mainland. On account of all the Neolithic monuments there, archaeologists call Rousay the Egypt of the North. I had come for a tomb called Knowe of Lairo. *Knowe* is an old word for a little hill, and so it is, but one made by people. The famous monuments of Mainland – Skara Brae, Maeshowe, Ring of Brodgar, Stones of Stenness – are thronged distractingly with tourists, by the busload. Knowe of Lairo, by dint of being on Rousay and therefore a boat trip beyond Mainland, is out of the way. It is a tapered mound of grass-covered earth on a terrace overlooking a stretch of water called Eynhallow Sound. The entrance is just a couple of feet square and demands a crawl through mud (the access to many Neolithic tombs is a grunting struggle). The chamber beyond, barely twice shoulder-width but more than 13 feet high, is built of slim sand-stone slabs, skilfully stacked like giant dominoes so that the space narrows to a pointed triangle as it reaches higher. Carefully crafted recesses either side held human bones. A fine-ground stone axe was found inside Knowe of Lairo some time between the wars, and some broken pottery. It is silent inside and cool. The tide of humankind flows elsewhere.

Rousay locals have mostly never been inside the tombs. They say when you grow up surrounded by them, the tombs are of no more interest than the ruined, abandoned cottages that also dot the fields. I think that is just what they say to strangers. I think it is more likely those folk were raised to respect the tombs, maybe to fear ghosts, and so kept their distance. As recently as 1911 an Orkney farmer reported how he had been digging into a burial mound on his farm when there appeared at his side an old man, grey-bearded, in tattered clothes. He had a warning for the farmer:

> Thou are working thy own ruin, believe me, fellow, for if thou does any more work, thou will regret it when it is too late. Take my word, fellow, stop working in my house, for if thou doesn't, mark my word, fellow, if thou takes another shuleful, mark my word, thou will have six of thy cattle dying in thy corn-yard at one time. And if thou goes on doing any more work, fellow – mark my word, fellow, thou will then have six funerals from the house, fellow; does thou mark my word; good-day, fellow.

According to the tale, the deaths of six cattle duly followed and the funerals of six members of the household.

I got talking to the farmer on whose land Knowe of Lairo sits. Among other things, he told me that in days gone by inhabitants of Orkney's smaller islands seldom felt the need to visit Mainland, let alone mainland Britain. Rousay was enough. Well within living memory one elderly lady made her first visit to the metropolis that is Kirkwall, Orkney's capital, when she needed to see a dentist for the first time. When she came home her family and neighbours were waiting to hear her impressions of the big city.

'There's nothing there but houses,' she said.

He told me too about a farmer who bought a new Land Rover and won a trip to London as a prize. He was flown south and met by a chauffeur who drove him round the city in a limousine. He saw Buckingham Palace, Tower Bridge, the British Museum and the rest. In the evening he was taken to a Soho nightclub for sophisticated entertainment. On his return to Rousay his friends asked if he had enjoyed it and would he ever go back.

'Ach, no,' he said. 'There's nothing there.'

It does a heart good to get a new angle on the world, see it through different eyes; to see that not all folk are drawn to the same centre of gravity.

Coldrum Stones is one of the names given to a Neolithic mound near the village of Trottiscliffe in Kent. It is also known as the Coldrum Long Barrow and the Adscombe Stones. This choice of names is symptomatic of uncertainty and forgetting. The Neolithic is out of reach in ways that will not be fixed. Fleeting memory has seen to it that the thinking of those first farmers cannot be known. The personality of that time has melted away.

Whatever you call Coldrum, it seems to be one of the first mounds raised by humankind in these islands. Radiocarbon dating says it is about 6,000 years old. Kent is still known as the Garden of England, its soil as fertile now as it was then. The trick of farming came here from Europe, and it is no surprise some of the earliest fields are close by the narrowest sea crossing.

Nowadays Coldrum is a rectangle of massive sarsen stones on top of a low ridge pointing east towards the Medway River. Sarsen is another old word, a corruption of the Old English *Saracen*, which means Arab or Muslim. It is a sort of silicified sandstone that once formed a brittle crust on the surface of much of southern England. Time and weather shattered the crust into pieces, some of them immovably huge. Such stones were a problem for farmers clearing land for fields they might plough. In this context, sarsen means anything awkward, uncooperative.

Coldrum has fared less well than Knowe of Lairo. It has been picked over like a corpse. Old-time Christians, convinced that it stood for ancient heathen ways, did all they could to unmake it; treasure hunters certain of gold and other treasure laid it lower still. The forlorn and roofless box of stone is all that remains of a chamber that was once the focal point of a long wedge of earth surrounded by a kerb of other sarsens. It is so dilapidated now it is hard to say much else for certain. There may have been a façade of sarsens in front of the mound's eastern end, a backdrop for forgotten ceremony. The chamber might have been topped by a capstone. The height and extent of the earth mound can only be guessed at. The Coldrum Stones have been excavated several times from the early nineteenth century onwards. The most modern analysis of bones recovered from the chamber suggests the remains of seventeen individuals were inside when it was closed for the last time long ago, between 4,000 and 5,000 years ago.

Because those Neolithic constructions usually contained some bones, they are always described as tombs. Churches and cathedrals have bones inside them too but are the venues for more than funerals. That the buildings the first farmers raised of stone and earth were likewise host to ceremonies to celebrate the living as well seems possible at least.

During its active life Coldrum may have cradled, for a long or a short time, other bones, more bones. Whatever else, whoever else, when its congregation decided to walk away from it for ever, only the remains of those seventeen were left inside – five men, four women, four teenagers, two younger children and two toddlers. It seems fair to say only a tiny proportion of the community's dead were ever placed inside the chamber. That so few human remains are ever found inside Neolithic tombs suggests the fate of most of the mortal remains of the early farmers was other than entombment. Archaeologists assume most of the dead were set aside in the landscape for wild animals and birds and other natural processes to take care of. Perhaps some were buried in scattered, forgotten graves. In any event, the tombs were apparently the final destination for only a few, chosen for reasons we cannot discern with any kind of certainty.

Entombed or not, whoever they were, they are all forgotten now, those farmers and builders. The bones of a handful were placed inside a building that had mattered for a while. Individuals were not laid out intact but jumbled like a game of pick-up sticks. The sample suggests an equality of sorts, 5,000 years ago. Maybe the individuals mattered in their time, held some status. Or was it chance that had their residency, their turn in the box, made permanent by a bigger decision to abandon the building while their bones were inside? Perhaps they were kings and queens, princes and princesses of their demesne. Maybe they were famous in their way. Famous or not, special or not, they knew violence. Three of the skulls – two of the women and one of uncertain sex – were fractured; two had healed in life while the third had taken an injury to the grave.

In the sparsely populated England of so long ago, people lived isolated from their fellows, separated by distances made difficult by forest and morass. Places like Coldrum may, by their prominence in the landscape, have broadcast, as it were, messages and meaning to those who passed them by, like a capsized yacht's EPIRB bleating in an empty ocean. *We are here . . . we are here . . .* The site is 500 yards or so from the Pilgrim's Way once used by Christians en route between the great churches of Winchester in Hampshire and Canterbury in Kent. The Pilgrim's Way is a more recent name and use for a prehistoric track so old it is impossible to date. It is the Old Road Hilaire Belloc called 'the most imperative and the first of our necessities'. The tracks made and followed by our ancestors were part of making sense of the landscape, making connections. Where once there was only wilderness, now there were ways to follow.

West Kennet in Wiltshire is among the most famous (and most visited) Neolithic tombs in England. A 330-foot-long sloped ridge of chalk rubble, it was also the resting place of just a few. Before its entrance was closed by massive sarsen blocks, West Kennet was another stage-set for ceremony. Archaeologists think it was open for worship for just a generation, maybe twenty-five years. During that time people came and went, sometimes leaving human bones, sometimes taking them away. The remains of men and women, young and old, were segregated between the chambers within. As at Coldrum, bodies were mostly not interred intact. More likely they were laid outside somewhere long enough for birds and scavengers to strip away the flesh. Only the sticky, stinking bones were gathered up and placed inside the tomb. I wonder were they, those folk, appalled by the stench of death, the corruption of their loved ones? They were no strangers to it. Separate piles were made of skulls and long bones, individuals subsumed into something bigger, a unified body of the ancestors.

It is strange and also intimate. Bones were handled and moved, over and over. Likely they were taken from the tomb from time to time for magic and meaning elsewhere. Maybe relatives took their loved ones home for visits. It was anyway a fellowship of death. When West Kennet was sealed shut for ever, the remains of just forty people were inside. Once, their existence in the world – even as dry bones – had something clear to say, part of an ongoing conversation. We are deaf to it now.

Those bones of Coldrum, of West Kennet, of Knowe of Lairo and the rest of the burial mounds are the voices of the Neolithic, but faded to whispers made only of our imaginings. Those individuals may have been the centre of attention, men and women both, known by their own and their descendants, their stories told and retold. They had been collected into a treasure box for safekeeping. It seems certain they were meant to be remembered. Now they are forgotten and utterly lost. However much they mattered – if they mattered – they are nameless for ever.

The attempt to remember is part of what makes us human, what sets us apart from other animals. The tide of forgetting is rising all the time. Those Neolithic farmers were few, numbering in the thousands. They edited their dead, keeping safe inside a box of stone a few of note and setting aside the rest. It was the most they could do. Intense though it may have been, even that remembering could not and did not last. The hope of being remembered after death is vanity. Vain or not, many of us in this twenty-first century are as fearful of being forgotten. When we are gone, and those who know us and love us now are gone too, we will be forgotten. It is that simple. Whoever we are, from highest to lowest, we do best to accept this well-proven truth while we get busy living.

Loch Doon
and light traces

Backward, turn backward, O Time, in your flight,
Make me a child again just for tonight!

— ELIZABETH AKERS ALLEN,
'Rock Me to Sleep'

HAVING NO TRAINING in the scientific method, and being all too aware of the limitations this places on my critical faculties, I value the company of scientists. In my line of work I have contact with specialists in many fields: biology, chemistry, physics, engineering, neuroscience, medicine . . . the list goes on. I mostly meet scientists while making television documentaries, and it is in the nature of filming that there are brief periods of activity dotted between long stretches of waiting around. It is while waiting that I ask scientists questions concerning concepts that puzzle me. These are many. Whenever I am with a specialist on the human brain I ask one question in particular: what does my wife's mobile telephone number look like inside my head?

I have read what I can bear of quantum theory, which is the science of very small things. QT suggests that entities behave one way when watched and another when not. Just as the unobserved universe is (according to QT) a cloud of possibility as opposed to things that are solid, constant, always there, so it seems the contents of the brain, the unconsciousness, might be similarly vague. So, when I am neither thinking about nor dialling my wife's phone number, what form does it take in the midst of the clutter?

In my imagination we have a microscope of limitless power and can use it to peer inside my noodle, trapped in solitary confinement inside my skull. What is a memory made of? I have asked this many times of different experts and their answers boil down to more or less the same thing: rather than existing in any sort of tangible form, safely filed in some ordered cabinet of the mind – a tiny string of digits in a clearly marked folder – my wife's number is another path, a way.

The first time I learned that eleven-digit number it was as though my mind had been a field of grass and I had walked a line through it. As I made my way through the numbers – 0 . . . 7 . . . 8 . . . – some stems were pressed flat. Had I only used the number once, the stems would have straightened again after I was gone, and any trace of the path would have disappeared. Through use and reuse of the number however, treading the path over and over, the stems eventually stayed flat, disinclined to rise. The path became permanent.

It is not, necessarily, a straight path. It may zig and zag like the pinging progress of a pinball. Whenever I need the number my consciousness retreads the path from beginning to end. If I should stop using it then the path might be lost, filled in as though it had never been.

I am interested in memory. Why do I remember the things I remember and why do I forget the things I forget? Some of what I remember seems arbitrary even to me, whose memories they are: glimpses of uneventful days; echoes of conversations that amounted to little; disconnected facts; snatches of song. I do not remember making paths of those remembrances and yet there they are, well-worn tracks. The

French philosopher Henri Bergson wrote in his 1896 work *Matter and Memory*, 'It is the function of the brain to enable us not to remember but to forget.' This must be true. We each of us experience, moment to moment, much more than might be committed to memory. Sights, sounds, smells, emotions, ideas – it is no wonder the brain is busiest with the business of clearing out the excess, so as to leave room for whatever titbits might be deemed worth keeping.

The Earth remembers too, after a fashion. After all the billions of years spent and lives lived there are traces left behind. Some of what has survived seems as unlikely, as ephemeral and as without significance as any human recollection.

In 1985, when I was eighteen, I took part in my first archaeological dig. It was on the shores of Loch Doon, near the market town of Dalmellington in the Carrick district of Ayrshire. We had gone there to investigate the chance discovery, some few years before, of some flakes of flint and chert left behind by Stone Age hunters. The scatter of flakes, known to archaeologists as debitage, were the debris left behind after the making of stone tools. The tools in question had been fashioned perhaps 8,000–9,000 years previously, during the Mesolithic – the middle Stone Age that followed the old Stone Age of the Palaeolithic. This was the time when the territory that would be Scotland was still waking up from the last ice age, when handfuls of people wrested lives from a wild world.

Our dig director, a charismatic and wonderful chap called Thomas Lamb Affleck, had selected for our four weeks of investigation some tens of square yards of ground close by the water. We would open up and carefully excavate several trenches, recording and photographing every scrap. Tom was a mature student, in his early sixties, having gone back to university in the 1970s to take a second degree. Previously he had studied botany (in years either side of service as a Spitfire pilot), been a market gardener and also a breeder of Irish wolfhounds and French bulldogs. He was unique and unforgettable, his quixotic, Rip

Van Winkle character defining a permanent path through the long grass of my brain.

Starr was how he had labelled the site, in honour of the nearby tumbledown cottage of the same name, in which we were lodging. As strongly as anything else I remember the smoke from the surly and uncooperative Rayburn stove we had for cooking.

It started raining during the second week and hardly stopped thereafter. Uncomfortable and miserable at first, things took a more significant turn when the water level of the loch began to rise. Inexorably the space between our carefully excavated trenches and the edge of the loch disappeared, an insidious process like forgetfulness come to steal from an elderly mind.

By way of a distraction from the inevitable, Tom led me away from the imperilled excavation and up on to a shelf of higher ground nearby. He had opened a trench there a year or two before. It had been little more than a keyhole, measuring perhaps 5 feet by 2. There was nothing to see on the ground now, the trench having been backfilled at the end of the season. Tucked under one arm, Tom had a scale plan he had made of the ground surface when it was briefly exposed. This he unrolled to show me the plottings he had made of every flake. At first glance it had the look of a piece of abstract art – hundreds of angular shapes smaller than fingernails and dotted like scattered confetti. I looked at the plan and then at Tom's face.

'Do you see the pattern?' he asked.

I looked again at the myriad shapes, like a snapshot of a field of asteroids in space, and shook my head.

He had me look again, and then carefully he pointed out two pairs of patches towards the middle of the plan that were completely blank, devoid of any flakes. There was a larger pair the size of beer mats and, a foot or so behind them, a smaller set.

I had not noticed the blanks until he pointed them out, but I was none the wiser for seeing them.

'That's where a flint knapper knelt down,' he said. 'The two bigger shapes were left by the knees, the smaller ones by the toes.'

I was then and remained ever after flabbergasted. Like much else from Loch Doon – Tom's effortless charm, the incessant rain, the smoke from the stove – I remember revelation. We could never know anything more about that person who had paused to put a sharp edge back on to a stone tool. We would never know if the work was undertaken by a man or by a woman. But with absolute certainty we knew where in the universe that person had knelt for a few minutes all those thousands of years ago. We also knew precisely what he or she had done with those moments of time. If I wanted I could place my hand where his or her knees had rested, his or her toes. After those minutes of labour that hunter stood up once more and walked away, into forever, disappearing utterly. How many times do you do something as inconsequential as kneel down – to retie a shoelace, to pick up something dropped? Imagine if, thousands of years from now, some stranger from a future unimaginable found a spot where you paused for a few moments, just that and no more. Imagine if that proof of those few moments was all the surviving evidence of your existence.

This in a nutshell is why archaeology appeals to me. History is made of words – books, letters, diaries, documents, gravestones. Stories made of words are informative but also biased, shaped by the author to make a point or favour one view over all the rest. Archaeology is the study of other things people leave behind. Some are made carefully and placed consciously so as to tell a story – a grave, a building, a work of art. Others are dropped by accident, lost inadvertently. Some, like those spaces left by knees and toes on a shelf of rock above Loch Doon, were made unconsciously and were never intended to be found. I have taken more meaning from those empty spaces than from anything else I saw while working as an archaeologist. More than anything else, those traces remind me that we cannot know which of our actions will matter. In 10,000 years you and yours, me and mine, will have disappeared. Likely nothing that seems dear to us will be remembered. Maybe, though, some infinitesimal act or gesture that seems utterly without consequence now will make all the difference in that world to come. However hard we might try, we do not choose if, far less how, we will be remembered. That much is for others to decide.

6.

Hunting

Peştera cu Oase
and eyes on the target

But my heart is a lonely hunter that hunts on a lonely hill.
Green is that hill and lonely, set far in a shadowy place,
White is the hunter's quarry, a lost-loved human face.

— WILLIAM SHARP,
'The Lonely Hunter'

THE AUSTRALIAN ARCHAEOLOGIST Vere Gordon Childe was first to imagine ancestors walking the Danubian Corridor. Once identified, it was accepted as having canalized and directed an endless flow. For millions of years, individuals from one branch of human life after another had been swept like twigs through the valleys and gorges of the Danube and Rhine rivers, north and west into the territory that became Europe. It was by following this line that *Homo erectus* found the way into Europe, and in the end all the way to the British Isles.

Homo sapiens was an explorer like all the rest, a wanderer gradually spreading around the globe. After the Middle East, some modern human beings turned east again, following a well-worn route to Asia and, ultimately, Australia and, via what is now the Bering Strait, the Americas. Who knows how far any one individual travelled in a lifetime? The movement of the species into the corners of the globe may have taken thousands of years of incremental advances – one more ridge climbed, one more river forded. Those that headed west made their way along the river valleys of Childe's Danubian Corridor, their descendants reaching the stretch that would one day be the border between Romania and Serbia. There they passed like argonauts through steep-sided narrows known as the Iron Gates.

As far as we know, modern humans like us did not penetrate the European continent until around 40,000 years ago. Members of our species were in what would become the Holy Land by perhaps as early as 177,000 years ago. Bone specialists discern as much from a partial jawbone found in Misliya Cave on Mount Carmel, near Haifa in Israel. Just part of the left upper jaw of a young adult, sex unknown and containing seven teeth, it has features (narrower in shape, taller forehead, less robust overall, more of a chin) that mark it out as different from the faces of Neanderthals known to have been in that part of the world at the same time or earlier. So near to Europe and yet, as it turned out, so far. Since it seems others of the same sort made it all the way to Australia, much further from Africa, by perhaps 60,000 years ago, it begs the question: what was blocking the way west for our ancestors?

For these ancestors, life depended at all times on acute awareness, competence and accuracy. Fear of danger had to be mastered if they were to bring down prey bigger than themselves. Given their ability and courage – and the promise of the rich hunting grounds of the European landmass – what kept them at bay for so long?

One explanation offered by archaeologists and palaeontologists is that the territory was already busy with human life, of at least one other species. The thinking goes that those *Homo sapiens* heading east may have kept to the coast, exploiting the marine environment as they went. This may have been a resource earlier incumbents – Neanderthals, *Homo erectus* et al. – had overlooked or eschewed. Since the youngest incomers had found a vacant niche, the coastline of the world beckoned, leading them further and further east. By contrast, progress into the interior of the European landmass demanded pursuit of animals and other provender into territory that may have already been claimed long ago. Highly competent Neanderthal hunters may have held sway. Bigger and stronger than *Homo sapiens*, long since physically adapted to a climate that was often periglacial and darkly demanding, their looming presence may have discouraged migration by prospectors from the south. Those newcomers, dark-skinned and hairless, may have shivered at the very thought of making inroads on a chilled world dominated by others.

A cache of wooden spears gradually excavated from a site in Schöningen, in Lower Saxony in Germany, between 1994 and 1998 were of a sophistication that put them on a par with modern javelins. Each was between 6 and 8 feet long, fashioned from spruce or pine. Their makers had learned to concentrate the weight in the front third of the spear, like those hurled by athletes today. Slender and lovely, they would have been lethal over distances in excess of 200 feet. They were made by Neanderthals. Here was evidence that transformed perceptions about the technical abilities of those previous stewards of the wild world. Spears of such quality meant hunters could attack and kill from a distance. Their manufacture and use implied hunting parties able to communicate in a detailed way, making forward plans for pursuing large, dangerous prey, and arming themselves appropriately. In short they revealed themselves as more modern, more *human*, than might previously have been thought. If it had ever seemed likely the Neanderthals were lumpen oafs, easily outwitted and ousted, then finds like the Schöningen spears forced a rethink. Perhaps their control of the hunting grounds of Europe was inviolate after all, lasting for thousands of years.

In time, the Danubian Corridor would be followed by the hunter-fishers who made their homes in Lepenski Vir. Later, they in turn would be displaced by farmers like those who had lived cheek by jowl with their neighbours at Çatalhöyük. Before temples, henges and circles of standing stones, before houses for the dead and the living, there were ways through the land that everyone knew, and unconsciously maintained through endless use.

On the other side of an ice age was the Europe of the Neanderthals. Although galloping science has shed light on their lives and times, they remain an enigma. Before their extinction their sort may have been abroad for half a million years, evolving down through the millennia and adapting to a changing world. Since we stumbled upon the first of their skeletons in 1856, in the Neander Valley near Düsseldorf, we have been mostly unkind in our talk of them. To accompany the heavy-set frame suggested by those first bones, we assumed the slothful, lumbering ways of the dullard. There has been a partial rehabilitation since, some reinvestment with dignity, but they remain stooped in our shadow. Still we keep them at a distance, deny them any kinship. They are the poor relations, and beneath us.

The Book of Genesis has skin in the game. While Rebekah, wife of Isaac, is pregnant with twins, God tells her she carries within her 'two manner of people . . . and the one people shall be stronger than the other people'. Esau was born first, the elder son. He was covered all over in red hair, 'like an hairy garment'. Before he could be lifted into his mother's arms, the younger son, Jacob, as yet unborn, thrust out an arm from within Rebekah's womb and grabbed Esau's heel, as though to hold him back. As they grew to manhood the twins were revealed as very different men. Esau was 'a cunning hunter, a man of the field' while Jacob was 'a plain man, dwelling in tents'. In time Jacob used all his wit and guile to cheat his elder brother out of his inheritance. Jacob gained all of their father's goods as well as his blessing. His usurpation of Esau was complete. Is this Bible story a fossil memory of what we did to the elder clade? Did we make ourselves feel better about denying the Neanderthals their inheritance, which was the world, by remembering them as monsters, trolls lurking in caves and under bridges?

In February 2002, cave divers crawled through flooded tunnels leading to subterranean galleries and chambers beneath the Iron Gates, close by the Romanian town of Anina. From a tiny space in a wall they felt a breath of air like an exhalation. Having excavated the space to make it wider, they wriggled one by one into a new place . . . which was also a very old place. They called the space they found Peştera cu Oase, Romanian for 'the cave with bones'. Archaeologists would find that the voids discovered by those cavers had been out of reach of humankind for 17,000 years. The bones, more than 5,000 of them, were of cave bears, wolves, goats – all sorts of mammals. Some of the bear bones had been carefully placed by people long ago, set up on rocks and ledges as though on natural altars. Nearby was found a human jawbone, the first of a whole collection of human remains. Radiocarbon dates suggested these human bones were around 38,000 years old – proof of the oldest modern humans in Europe.

Peştera cu Oase was already a place of wonder when bone experts realized they were dealing with the remains of a hybrid – a mixing of the DNA of *Homo sapiens* and *Homo neanderthalensis*. The first hints had been in the bones themselves: one jawbone had a chin, a characteristic of modern faces; the forehead of another skull lacked the brow ridge so definitive of Neanderthals. So far, so modern – and yet, and yet . . . other fragments of bones suggested something else. While they appeared modern in the main, there was something old about them too. The results of the DNA analysis revealed that at least one of the Peştera cu Oase bones had such long stretches of Neanderthal code plaited through it the individual could only be four to six generations removed from the original coupling of Neanderthal and Modern.

We have known for a while that there was interbreeding of the species at some point: all modern European people have Neanderthal

DNA in their code. The remains from the Cave of Bones carry us unexpectedly close to one of those unions. Present thinking has allowed for the possibility it was the mixing of those two species that made all the difference in the world; that made us what we are. Neither the original marque of *Homo sapiens* out of Africa nor the Neanderthals held the keys to the future. It seems possible, even likely, that it was the mongrel dog they made together that learned the best tricks.

Hybrids happen behind Mother Nature's back. While she has in place mechanisms to keep species distinct from one another, some of her offspring take chances as they present themselves. When a male donkey mates with a female horse, the occasional consequence is a mule. Mules are usually sterile, male mules especially; where the offspring is female, she might be fertile. Mules are famously smarter, more loyal, healthier and more stubborn than either horses or donkeys. Mules are a desirable result of the mixing of species.

Hunters hunt. At all times they must be on the look-out for possible targets. Life itself is a hunter, and the ultimate target, the prime objective, is more life, made by the coming together of male and female, mating and the production of offspring.

Somewhere along the Danubian Corridor, a *Homo sapiens* heading north and west encountered a Neanderthal. Maybe the former was a man, the latter a woman: we cannot know which way the cards fell. They came together and at least one of the products of their coupling was fertile. How much closer to the story of Adam and Eve do we need to get? Somewhere out there – ground to dust no doubt – are the bones of them.

We have wandered a long way since the days of the Danubian Corridor. The things that once held our species in awe are diminished. Even the highest place on Earth, Mount Everest, is somehow beneath us. An older name for the peak is Chomolungma, meaning Goddess Mother of the Earth. When that name mattered it was a sin even to trespass on her flanks, far less seek the summit. Now the climbers' base camp is a rubbish dump. Everywhere we go we leave a mess; everything we touch we eventually defile.

Somewhere out there our Eve, mother of all of us, lies lost beyond the finding. We have strayed so far from our natural selves we do not even recognize our own mother, far less miss her. We must open our eyes and see her where she has been all along – all around us. Sooner or later we must seek her forgiveness and begin to make amends.

Chauvet Cave
and a kingdom of animals

She explained that it was only when the people of
the early race snatched fire from underneath the
wing of the great ostrich ancestor of all the
ostriches and started using it for their own selfish
ends that the animals took fright and ran away
from human beings. But even though they fled they
never forgot the meaning of the sound in which
they had first conversed in harmony with men.

— LAURENS VAN DER POST,
A Story Like the Wind

ACCORDING TO THE *Encyclopaedia Britannica*, 'the first complete tradition in the history of art' hails from a part of the Palaeolithic (the old Stone Age) called the Aurignacian. A span of some 20,000 years, the period is named after the Cave of Aurignac in the town of that name in the Haute-Garonne department of southern France, where the traces of that past time were first glimpsed. The hunters who used the cave were of the sort archaeologists used to call Cro-Magnon – after that other cave, the Abri de Cro-Magnon in Les Eyzies. The five thirty-millennia-old skeletons found there suggested people of a robust and powerful sort. They were the first of us, the Cro-Magnons, the first fully modern humans in Europe. No one knows for sure, but their sort was likely out and about upon the continent from 40,000 years ago, or more. For at least the first 10,000 years of their tenancy they shared the place with Neanderthals.

Those Cro-Magnons were in Europe during the warm years between the last two ice ages. Like the Neanderthals before them, they made use of many caves. In the limestone caves of France, sinuous, serpentine spaces made and left behind aeons ago by fast-flowing water, they made art. What that art reveals, the answer it offers up to the question of what it means to be alive, is that the first of us knew and understood their place within a kingdom of animals.

In December 1994 a trio of potholers, one Jean-Marie Chauvet among them, made their way to the pinched, mean mouth of an entrance into a rock wall in the Ardèche region of southern France, close by a massive natural limestone arch called Le Pont d'Arc. That they had come there at all was down to Chauvet's friend and fellow spelunker Michel Rosa, known to *ses amis* as Baba. In the spring of the same year, Baba had felt air flowing from the aperture and guessed at the existence of caves beyond. He could gain no access but told Chauvet what he had discovered. It was Chauvet who returned at the end of the year with two other friends. What they found ought to have been known as Le Trou de Baba, 'Baba's Hole', but it is the Chauvet Cave instead.

The Cro-Magnons, who came that way seeking darkness tens of millennia before, surely looked up at the arch and saw in it the outline of a mammoth's humped back. Spurred on by the sight, they sought the underworld there. The access they had to the cave was not the tiny aperture breached by Chauvet and co. but another, older, easier way blocked twenty-odd thousand years ago by a rockslide. But for as long as that way remained open, it was a portal to another world. Inspired or not by the animal-arch, they left the light behind – light that fell, in their world, on the backs of mammoths, cave lions, bears 12 feet tall and that giant deer called megaloceros whose antlers were as wide as the spreading branches of a tree.

It seems those artists, those hunters, never made any sort of home in the cave. Entering only in reverence, or perhaps in fear, they came from time to time to summon animals from the rock. As well as stalking them in the world above, they sought some other essence of their fellow travellers in the world below, and so the hunt began in the womb of the world. They made fires there and prepared charcoal for drawing. They powdered red ochre for the colour of blood and life. By the light of lamps and tapers they found surfaces that seemed right and touched them and so made animal spirits rise to where they could see them and outline them with blackened fingers and brushes made of horsehair. They took advantage of undulations in the living rock – signs of life beneath – to evoke muscle and movement as they watched and rendered lions hunting giant wild cattle, sketched unsuspecting families of bears, and unleashed torrents of galloping horses and ibex – a carnival of animals flooding over the rock like the water that had smoothed the walls long before.

Chauvet is frozen time where the ashes of fires that died 30,000 years ago still lie at peace. In the dust on the floor are footprints made by Cro-Magnon men, women and children. On the walls are scratches made by bear claws, and on the floor hollows where those great beasts wintered. Archaeologists have recovered 150 bear skulls from the cave – bears having inhabited the space from time to time. As affecting as the figurative art are many patches of red ochre, in rows and clumped in groups. Two Cro-Magnons, one smaller one larger, one with a crooked finger, took turns to cup handfuls of the dampened pigment and splat it on to the rock. Their thoughts and touch are close there in the time-stalled dark.

Cro-Magnon, *Homo sapiens*; we might be the first animals to have known we are animals. This has been a predicament. We are aware of ourselves and of time, of beginning and ending. Alone among the animals, we are driven to ask why. Why anything? It seems likely they saw little if any separation between themselves and their four-legged fellows – brother bear, sister lion. Some of the profiles, the lions especially, have something human about them, a fusion of species. Would-be writers are told to write what they know; hunters must know who they hunt.

The hunters of the Palaeolithic were animal and human in a kingdom of animals. They were vulnerable at all times, moment to moment. Life was water held in their cupped hands. They were outnumbered, hugely, by a host of creatures stronger and faster than themselves. But while they were ready prey for lion and wolf and the rest of the waiting tooth-and-claw predators, those humans were uniquely skilled. They could run and carry. They could imagine weapons and therefore make them. Rather than grapple with beasts they could stand back, or wait in branches above and send death via the end of a spear, or an arrow shaft.

If there ever was a time when the animals spoke a language the hunters understood, then surely it was then. Among so much else we do not know, we cannot say for certain when the speech of humankind was separated from the song and sounds made by other animals. We cannot divine when our kind began to use language and words for making plans and sharing ideas.

They had fire, coaxed from wood on wood by fast and clever hands, and so could keep the beasts at bay with flames, or panic them into reckless flight towards readied traps and the edges of precipitous cliffs. Vulnerable our ancestors surely were, but they were dangerous in their own right. They were predators too, hunters, and above all else they knew their survival and that of their kin depended upon knowing the target, approaching the target and striking the target. Failure to hit the target was in every sense a matter of life and death.

It is from the Latin *erro* that we get our English verb 'to err'. *Erro* is close, linguistically, to the Sanskrit *arsati* and the proto-Indo-European *ers*: both mean 'to wander around'. In all cases there is a sense of aim-lessness, literally a lack of aiming. The Greek verb *hamartano* means 'to miss the target' – specifically in relation to the throwing of spears. In the Greek form of the New Testament, *hamartano* and *hamartia* (which is the noun form) are used to mean 'sinning' and 'sin', a weakness or flaw that leads to downfall. In this context, 'to sin' is to miss the target. For us, sinning came to mean doing wrong in the eyes of God. But follow the roots deep enough and it turns out that the original sin, as far as hunters like the Cro-Magnons in the Aurig-nacian Palaeolithic were concerned, was failure to hit something with a spear.

We would understand so much more if we knew and understood the roots of our words. It seems to me important to notice that our most distant ancestors were wrestling with deep thoughts, trying to understand, hunting for meaning. For as long as there has been writing, people have recorded a version of a story in which a figure, a hero, leaves behind family and all else he knows. He makes his way into the underworld and there fights the unknown, in whatever manifestation, in order to free his father from the darkness. Having reclaimed his father he returns to the light with the wisdom to set the world aright. The story is older than writing. We have no way of knowing how long people have sat around a fire and listened to a storyteller describe the striving of the hero who travels into the underworld in search of meaning.

Tens of thousands of years ago in a wild world, while ice ages waxed and waned, hunters knew there was more to life than that which they could see and feel in the everyday. Beset by dangers and challenges unimaginable to us, still they were driven to seek answers. Some of them ventured into the dark and used fire and art to summon the spirits of the animals they lived among and depended upon. Having brought them to the surface of the rock, watched their movements stretch that rock into humps and sinuous curves, they traced the lines of them in black and red. They were seeking to take control, to see the targets their lives depended upon. Even now, in spite of all we have learned and know, we still lack direction and will only wander without aim if we are not certain of our targets.

Carnac Stones
and paying attention

To return to the stones of Carnac (or rather, to leave
them), if anyone should, after all these opinions . . .
ask me mine, I would emit an irresistible,
irrefutable, incontestable one . . . This is my opinion:
the stones of Carnac are simply large stones!

— GUSTAVE FLAUBERT,
Over Strand and Field

PRESERVATION OF THE past is a modern predilection. For as
long as there has been speech, people have told each other stories,
including stories about the past – real or imagined. With writing came
the means permanently to record that which had previously only been
committed to memory. Herodotus, Xenophon, Polybius, Caesar – there
is a long list of historians from the centuries BC onwards. But the desire
to stop time around certain places and things – to conserve and keep
them hermetically sealed – is a much more recent development.

By the time English antiquarian William Stukeley was paying close
attention to the Avebury Stones, in the early 1720s, the villagers there
were feverishly busy taking the place apart. For want of any other explanation, the circles were often explained as the work of some mischief or

other – giants turned to stone, scenes set for witchcraft. Since the stones were usually assumed to be the work of Godless heathens of one sort or another, they were fit only to be undone, pushed over, shattered by fire and quarried for the building of decent Christian homes. It is thanks to Stukeley that the monument survived at all, if without many of its menhirs. Similar tales can be found all over these islands – this Churchman or that whipping up his congregation into a froth of righteous anger over ancient sites and encouraging their destruction. Who knows how much was done away with? It is our habit now to preserve cathedrals, carefully maintaining them at great expense. Yet in the past it was common practice for a new archbishop to level the old house of God and have a newer, better replacement raised in its place. Sentimental our forebears were not.

The accounts of seventeenth- and eighteenth-century antiquarians are rich with discoveries of caves filled with bones of ancient animals – mammoths, sabre-toothed cats, rhinos and the like – left untouched for millennia. When the Reverend William Buckland climbed down into Goat's Hole Cave on Yellow Top Headland at Paviland, on the Gower, in January 1823, he found the floor within littered with remains of ancient fauna and thought them proof of creatures drowned in the Flood. Yet it was not just animal bones that lay in wait in spaces out of sight. In 1797, two men digging out a rabbit burrow near Burrington Combe in the Mendip Hills in Somerset broke through, inadvertently, into a cave. Laid out in rows, in serried ranks across the floor, were human skeletons, a hundred or more. And then . . . nothing. Apparently content with no more than a story to tell down the pub, the pair saw no reason to invest the place with any meaning. Not until 1860 did William Boyd Dawkins bother to take another look, widening the entrance and naming the find Aveline's Hole after his mentor and fellow antiquarian William Talbot Aveline. And it was not until 1914 that any proper archaeological investigation was carried out, by which time only twenty-one of the skeletons remained (assuming the rabbit hunters had their initial tally right). These were stored in the Bristol Museum until a November night in 1940 when a Luftwaffe bomb blew much of the assemblage into the sky. Only in recent years were the fragments examined and found to be Mesolithic hunters (slight of build, leaving scant trace of their passage) who lived and died between 10,000 and 11,000 years ago.

Near the village of Thetford on the Suffolk–Norfolk border are the Neolithic flint mines called Grime's Graves. Those ways into the underground were noticed more than a thousand years ago – the name was applied by Anglo-Saxons and reveals that they thought them quarries dug by Grim, their hooded god. Only in the latter part of the nineteenth century were they properly investigated (by Churchman and archaeologist William Greenwell) and found to be shafts to mines where farmers had burrowed deep 5,000 years ago in search of flint for axe blades. Leaning against the chambers' walls, just as they had been left, were picks made of deer antler. Earthquakes and landslides had shut the door on more, the rest left in peace for several millennia.

It seems that for the longest time our forebears went about their business in landscapes littered with monuments, artefacts and bones, and either were oblivious to their presence or thought them of no consequence. Aside from the damage inflicted under the influence of religious zeal, proof of the past was left alone. Maybe lives were too hard until recently, all the hours of the day taken up with chores and none left over for idle prospecting for forgotten things in dusty alcoves.

In the fields north of Carnac, Brittany, in the Morbihan region of north-west France, there are thousands of standing stones stretching in lines more than a mile long, set in place maybe 6,000 or 7,000 years ago – no one is sure. As well as the stones there are tumuli and dolmens, places for keeping safe the remains of the dead.

The stone rows, often disappearing out of sight over the horizon, are beguiling. Rather than parallel lines, they form patterns more like veins. Stand among them and it is easy to be mesmerized. However they were arranged in the beginning, what is there now is the result of modern interference and restoration. Time had seen to the toppling of many, if not most. Earthquakes may have played their part, shaking the monoliths loose from their sockets like old men's teeth.

Some attention was paid to the stones in the eighteenth century, and there were all sorts of ideas to explain them – suggestions that the lines had been foundations for a druid university, or sights through which one might watch the movement of stars. A French engineer by the name of Monsieur de la Sauvagère suggested Caesar had the stones raised to support his soldiers' tents. The French novelist Gustave Flaubert visited Carnac in May 1847, reviewed the various interpretations and decided no more could or should be said but that they were 'simply large stones'.

In the 1860s a Scottish antiquarian called James Miln turned his attention to those large stones and noted how few remained standing. He employed a local lad, Zacharie Le Rouzic, as his assistant. As much as anything else, Miln was impressed by the apparent tenacity of the tribes that had raised them. In *Excavations at Carnac* he wrote, 'One is tempted to ask how it is that the Romans, masters of the world, came and disappeared, whilst the race of the crude constructors still remains.'

After Miln's death Rouzic went further, setting the stones upright once more. There has been more rearrangement since. In the 1930s and again in the 1980s stones were moved to make way for a thoroughfare. In 1991 the Heritage Ministry stepped in and raised gated fences around the stones to restrict public access (ironically more stones were moved then too, to make way for grim green chain links). In 2002 a protest group calling itself the Everyone Together Collective seized the keys and threw open the gates. Safe to say it has all been a bit of a mess – well-meaning in parts perhaps, but it is anyone's guess how much the setting of the Carnac Stones now resembles that of all those thousands of years ago. Subtleties in the thinking of the builders are surely lost. By merely setting stones upright in approximations of the original design we do no more than mimic the past, parroting sounds we do not understand.

Tourists and visitors to Carnac come and go. Some days the rows are mobbed with wanderers and wonderers. When I visited a few years ago, I too was amazed by them. It is not until you are confronted by the sheer number of granite boulders of every shape and size that the scale of the ancient ambition hits home. However they were placed, and for whatever reason, they are at least testament to humbling effort.

I was guided around the stones and the tombs by French archaeologist Serge Cassen, who suggested that the rows were the work not of farmers but of hunters. Brittany was likely free of ice during the last ice age, meaning the hunting way of life, the first way of life of our species, may have continued unbroken there for tens of thousands of years, if not longer. Those who had lived by harvesting wild game and food from land and sea, whose ancestors had clung to the territory (in small numbers, admittedly) even as the ice sheets moved elsewhere, found their world encroached upon by incomers with revolutionary ideas. Farmers from the north and east, the vanguard of a great wave of change, arrived in search of land to cultivate, to feed their flocks and herds.

Cassen's idea was moving, but whimsical. It seemed at least possible to him that the beleaguered hunters, trapped with their backs to the sea, had raised the stones in defiance, as visible proof of their determination to be seen and respected. His point got me thinking. Perhaps their defiance had mattered after all. Perhaps those hunters took the whip hand, made themselves masters of the incomers. Maybe it was hunters that put those farmers to work – tending rented fields and raising rows of stones. It is true to say that hunters still rule the roost in our islands. Who plants and harvests and husbands the animals while men and women on horseback, clad in rich red, go hunting through those same fields? What is the still-championed sport of aristocrats and other landowners, while their tenants plough the fields and tend the domesticated beasts?

The stone rows of Carnac are the greatest of their kind, but similar forms can be found elsewhere on continental Europe and also in the British Isles. There are avenues of stone like those leading to Avebury from henges nearby. Better still, if on a much smaller scale than Carnac, are stone rows in Caithness and Sutherland. More than twenty sites have been recorded there, the most impressive being the Hill o' Many Stanes south of Wick, where some 200 stones around 3 feet high are arranged in a fan on the slopes of a south-facing hill. Attempts at interpretation have been made there too, but mostly to no avail.

The Carnac Stones are still under threat, according to protesters intent on their survival. Little by little they are encroached upon, or subject to neglect. Their circumstances might act as a warning; so too the predicament of all manner of traces of our past. Stonehenge, the most famous of all the monuments of the UK, is set to have a tunnel burrowed beneath it. Elsewhere there are calls for the destruction of statues and memorials to actors in other parts of our nation's stories – Horatio Nelson, Winston Churchill and the like. Murals of moments are painted over or otherwise defaced. This is the erasing of the past. It is always easiest of all to forget, or to pretend it never happened in the first place.

Some ancient sites and historic buildings are fossilized, time stopped in their vicinity. But always in the background is the temptation to demolish and start over. Any builder will tell you it is quickest, easiest and cheapest to knock down an old house and build anew rather than take the trouble to absorb the expense of restoring the original. With every demolition and erasing we lose some part of the truth of ourselves, good or bad.

For hope and inspiration I look to the hunter mindset, as imagined by Serge Cassen at Carnac. The act of remembering is one of defiance in the face of passing time. We live now in a world in which the pace of change is increasing drastically. More and more we service machines that are soon to be much cleverer than us. The hard drives and servers record and store, but they do not remember. Remembrance must be suffused with meaning or else all we will have is data, which is not the same. In order to keep in touch with ourselves and to understand how we got to where we are it is necessary – vital – to remember. We must be hunters, hunting down the past, all that remains, and know it intimately like a hunter understands his prey. The evidence is an endangered species. It would be a dangerous mistake to assume the past will survive on its own, that it will always be there to refer to. Look at how much has already been forgotten, now lost for ever. Whole ways of thinking, ways of making sense of what it means to be a human being alive in the universe, are lost in the shadow of stones whose meanings we cannot read. Our prey is putting distance between us because our eyes are elsewhere. The Ancient Egyptians who raised the mightiest stones of all, the pyramids, surely assumed their meaning would always be understood, but no. The stones survive, but their story is gone for good.

The past is a foreign country, as L. P. Hartley rightly said. The past is the book that records the steps to where we are now – and the missteps. It is also fragile as gossamer, likely to be brushed away. There are plenty of missing pages already. We cannot leave it to others, far less to machines, to do the job of remembering. Each of us must do our bit, hunt down some part of the past that comprises the whole.

Remembering matters. In all of the universe, so far as we know, remembering is uniquely human. We must not take it for granted. We must pay attention.

7.

Reaching

Utyevka Kurgan
and life always on the move

There are pioneer souls that blaze their paths
Where highways never ran . . .

— SAM WALTER FOSS,
'The House by the Side of the Road'

O N THE FLOODPLAIN of the Samara River, a tributary of the Volga River, the landscape is marked by manmade mounds. The local name for these is *kurgan*, a word with roots in East Slavic and all the way down to some lost tongue of the Turkic family of languages spoken across Eurasia. Kurgans are burial mounds, and there by the river they form cemeteries made and used by nomadic pastoralists – herders of sheep and cattle – as many as 5,000 years ago. There are numerous kurgans on the swathe of territory known vaguely as the Russian steppe – hundreds of thousands of them.

A kurgan, generally speaking, is a circular mound of earth heaped over a deep rectangular chamber or pit. Sometimes the borrowed space was lined with timber, sometimes not. The majority of kurgans started out as markers for the remains of just one individual. Before the chamber was backfilled and the mound heaped upon it, the body was usually covered in red ochre, or accompanied by raw lumps of the stuff, which explains the preference of some archaeologists for the name Ochre Grave Culture. Sometimes only the skull was interred. Burials are often accompanied by finery – weapons, jewellery, sacrificed animals, chariots and other wheeled vehicles. Often, over time, more bodies were inserted into the mound.

On the floodplain of the Samara, close by the village of Utyevka, archaeologists investigated four kurgan cemeteries. A mound they named Utyevka cemetery 1, kurgan 1 was found to be splendid. Measuring around 360 feet across, it represented a huge physical effort on the part of the herders who gathered and paused to build it. Inside the chamber was the skeleton of an adult man – dear to them? Feared by them? Who knows? In typical fashion, he had been laid down on his back. It was difficult to say exactly how his legs had been positioned when he first went into the ground but more than likely his knees were hitched chin-wards into a semblance of the foetal position. With him, for his aggrandizement in the hereafter, were two gold rings unlike any others found for thousands of miles around, a dagger of copper, an iron-headed copper pin, two different types of copper axe head, a copper awl and a pestle made of polished stone. Whoever he was – a chief, a beloved father and grandfather, a revered elder – he died and was entombed around 2500 BC, more or less the same time some farmers set themselves to raising the great sarsen trilithons of Stonehenge.

It may seem strange to mention, in this context, Britain's most famous ancient monument, but the people who buried a great man of theirs at Utyevka were part of a flow that would reach England and beyond, bringing new technologies and a new understanding of the world that would alter the destiny of all. They may have carried as well a hidden passenger, a microscopic stowaway capable of wreaking havoc.

In much of the more recent literature, the word Yamnaya is prominent. *Yamna* or *yamnaya* is Russian for a pit – hence Yamnaya Culture.

Hailing from what we call southern Russia and eastern Ukraine, the Yamnaya were herders of cattle. They were also among the first in the world to tame and ride the horses that roamed wild over the steppe. As well as riding them, they had the beasts accept the burden of hauling wagons and so they were highly mobile, carrying their worldly goods across the globe. Where they ventured into wintry terrain, on the endless search for grass, their high-stepping horses were equipped for breaking through snow cover to reveal the fodder preserved beneath.

Pollen cores from the soil of the middle Volga region reveal a changing climate there between 3500 and 3000 BC, from wetter to drier. The steady desiccation of the steppes made the grass coverage less complete, less reliable. People dependent on and responsible for cattle had to keep on the move from pasture to pasture. Once the Yamnaya had horses and wagons, they were free to follow the sun all the way into the west. They had weapons as well as wagons and it has been assumed they were of a warlike disposition. Powerful men, men of exceptional will, they rose above their fellows. As well as horsemen and warriors, they were among those minded to bury their dead in pits beneath great mounds.

The ceaseless roaming meant different tribes were forever encountering one another on the back and forth, and to smooth the way and sidestep trouble a common language evolved, a mother tongue. Those who understood one another might share some fledgling sense of identity. It was in this way, according to linguists, that the so-called proto-Indo-European (PIE) languages were summoned into being.

Cattle, too, were always entwined with humans. Cows yield more milk than mares or sheep and so were prized, even worshipped. The Yamnaya had acquired the necessary tolerance for lactose and were devoted to their cattle. The ability to digest lactose is derived from a mutation that occurred in people living west of the Ural Mountains around 6,500 years ago. Anyone alive today enjoying milk, cheese and yoghurt owes the adaptation to descent from those like the Yamnaya. Cattle were accumulated by the mighty – great herds symbolic of wealth and power. Daughters might be sold into marriage if a suitor offered enough cows as the price. The earliest PIE has roots in Sanskrit, and the Sanskrit for 'war' means, literally, 'the hunger for more cows'. 'Chattel', which is close to 'cattle', is the earliest word for any kind of personal property.

And so the Yamnaya rode over the steppe, driving their beasts before them, hauling the stuff of their lives and hailing one another in tongues alike enough to be mutually understood. Silent within, as yet unspoken, were the first languages of these islands: Gaelic and Irish, Welsh and Cornish, *British*. When they had to, those wanderers paused, gathering to raise kurgans over the graves of the greatest among them. Sometimes they slaughtered many horses as part of the funeral rite – enough to feed thousands at the feast – and buried the heads alongside the godfather. The temporary lodgings they raised for themselves, tented villages surrounded by their wagons, left hardly a trace. It was only with their dead that they made permanent marks upon the whispering vastness that was their world.

The PIE languages reveal a society, an ordering of people's lives, based around men, fighting men. Perhaps most of those riding west in search of new lands were men anyway, taking for wives those women they encountered on the way. Perhaps skilled warriors offering defence and therefore security in a wild world made for desirable mates. Words for father, grandfather, husband and brother – specifically in the context of inheritance – are more common and have deeper roots than those entitling wives, mothers, grandmothers and sisters. Most of those deemed deserving of a kurgan burial were men. That patriarchal tendency came out of the east, out of the eastern steppe, bundled among the rest of the cargo loaded on their wagons.

It was into the west, inexorably, that they came. Western Europe was a world of farmers by then, millions of farmers in settled communities rearing crops and animals. The lives they lived they had inherited from the light-skinned, dark-eyed people who had flowed through Anatolia to the valley of the Danube past Lepenski Vir and onwards into the west. Over centuries, millennia, they had sought to understand what it meant to be alive in the cosmos. It was the striving that had made them. Where their dead were gathered together in tombs there were men and women both, a seeming equality. When the PIE languages began to spread they reflected the difference at first – a different approach to the sexes between those of the west and those of the east.

Some time in the early centuries of the third millennium BC, east came west. Those of the kurgan, the Yamnaya and their ilk, were in search of pasture. To reach the long island of Britain they made boats, there being no other way. They encountered the settled farmers in their villages. In the Orkney Islands the wanderers found folk distracted, preoccupied with cutting great circles into bedrock and raising shards of stone towards the sky. It was the same at the other end of the long island, at Stonehenge and Avebury, where coveted grass grew upon chalk white as bone. At scores of other sites besides, people came together in their thousands to do and build likewise. What must the incomers have thought of those ways? What do nomads ever really think of those who always stay home?

According to archaeologists who have studied the teeth of 500 skeletons exhumed from Russia (and also Croatia, Estonia, Germany, Hungary and Latvia), those Yamnaya migrants may have brought with them more than language and metal weapons. Wound around the DNA of six of them were telltale twists of *Yersinia pestis*, the ancestor of the Black Death bacterium. Millennia before the pandemics of more recent history a form of the plague was endemic among the peoples of the steppe. While they had learned to live with it, the peoples of the west to whom it was unknown had not. Like the indigenous populations of the Americas that had no immunity to smallpox or even the common cold, and so died in droves on contact with the Europeans of the sixteenth century, so the Neolithic farmers of western Europe 4,000-5,000 years ago were hopelessly vulnerable to the incomers' travelling companion.

Whether or not they were harvested by plague, their ancient way of life was altered, subsumed. By the close of the third millennium BC the west was changing beyond recognition. Farming settlements, long established and hitherto thriving, fell away. There was a harrowing, a thin time. Populations contracted for hundreds of years. Only after perhaps half a millennium did numbers rise again. In the north, as far west as the Rhine, there grew a predilection for a pottery decorated by winding a cord around the wet clay. Vessels so impressed, called Corded Ware, became a commonplace in graves especially.

Analysis of the DNA of some of those buried with Corded Ware pots revealed they were people from the east, or their descendants. There in the double helix of those dead were found markers that set them apart from the older, indigenous Europeans. And so the vast majority of modern inhabitants of Europe have the genes of the incomers, the migrants – the Yamnaya who came out of the east 5,000 years ago. What of those older inhabitants – those that had built the tombs and cut the circles, who had been tenants of the west for thousands of years? The science is not yet conclusive. It is not yet possible to say the sitting tenants fully succumbed to a plague spread among them by immigrants. The most recent clues provided by the analysis of DNA, however, at least hint at a replacement of one by the other. A time to reap and a time to sow. However it happened, western Europe went through an upheaval as slow-moving as a glacier but as massive and as irresistible.

Suggestions of disruptive folk movements in prehistory have often upset archaeologists, who prefer to think of ideas on the move instead of people; always the hope of a past Utopia when people were better, kinder to each other. Invasions – flooding by the foreigner, the 'other' – are unsettling to contemplate. But people have been on the move from the beginning. The oldest grave in the British Isles containing metal is that of the so-called Amesbury Archer buried near Stonehenge around the time when that monument was in its final phase 4,500 years ago. Along with the stone wrist guards, worn to protect his forearm from the rebound of a bow string, and sixteen flint arrowheads that were all that remained of a quiver of arrows (hence the 'archer' epithet), he was sent into forever with three copper knives and two pieces of gold jewellery worn in long hair. He was also accompanied by a 'cushion stone' of the sort used by a smith to finish metal items. They lined his grave with timber and laid him down on his side with his knees drawn up to his chin. Perhaps he had asked them to do so, in memory of elsewhere. Analysis of his teeth showed the Amesbury Archer had had his childhood not in southern England but somewhere south of the Alps. He came here as an adult. Strangers were on the move thousands of years ago, bringing new skills like metal-working, new fashions, new languages, new rules, new religions, new ways of being. The man buried at Amesbury, the stranger with the skill of making metal things, may have ridden a wave already rising on the continent. Modern Europeans are likely descended from the kurgan-builders and from those among the light-skinned, dark-eyed farmers that went before them and survived the plague when it came.

Upsetting, unsettling – it makes no difference. People have moved across the globe from the beginning and often, as determined as locusts or an invading army. Reaching out for the horizon and beyond is a driving force of human nature. Laying claim to what was previously enjoyed by someone else is either an act of violation or in the natural order of things – dependent only on a person's point of view. Occupation of a place is never for ever. The longer a population has stayed in place, the tighter the bonds of the community rooted there, the more painful the disruption wrought by new arrivals with new ideas. From Yamnaya to

Far-off Fårö

and the journeys that matter

Yes, stretch out your hands into infinity
you human things.
Past blind moons and ice cream worlds
You hurl your metal ball of dull intelligence
And show us all our fragile grip.

— BOB GELDOF,
'Thinking Voyager 2 Type Things'

FROM HIGH ABOVE Orkney Mainland, as an astronaut might see it, that hub of the archipelago has the look of a featherless chick fallen from its nest – outsize head and beak to the west, stubby wings and tail to the east. Go back 12,000 years and the sea was lower, more of Orkney proud of the seal splash, whale crash. There has been a drowning since then. No doubt the hunters noticed, and so witnessed the theft of the land their grandparents walked upon. As well as home for those already there, it has been (and remains) a destination for others who glimpsed the hope of it from far away, an end of journeys.

For two and a half centuries or so, since 1783 and Étienne Mont-golfier and his hot air balloon flight, we have had the chance to look down on Earth from above. Before that our ancestors had a different angle and saw their own meaningful shapes with hunters' eyes. Where that fallen chick's eye would be there are two lochs, fresh Harray and salty Stenness. They are kept apart, yin and yang, by a finger of land, the narrow way between them. At the southern end of the isthmus are stepping stones through a slither of brackish water. For a long time, the gap has been bridged for motor vehicles. A few yards from the crossing, on a table top of higher ground towards the east and the rising sun, is the monument called the Standing Stones of Stenness. All around those stones like shards fallen from space, around those lochs, is what they call the Heart of Orkney, with its UNESCO World Heritage status. Nearby, beyond the other end of the isthmus, is a second circle, the Ring of Brodgar. The burial mound of Maeshowe is minutes away on foot, a pregnant, grassy bump. A thousand years ago its promise of buried treasure lured Vikings. Inside they insolently scratched their runes and beasts on smooth stones that had kept watch over bones much older than their kind. Towards the middle of the isthmus, at the finger's middle knuckle, is the Ness of Brodgar where Neolithic farmers spent a thousand years raising buildings for both shelter and worship, and razing them down again when they did not suit. Farmers know better now than to dig too deep in fields for fear of finding more and inviting on to their land an infestation of archaeologists.

Orkney is overwhelming, seemingly made of more than three dimensions. Weather is a shaping force, a time lapse of scudding clouds and swelling light, swords of gold and silver lancing from behind cover of bruised shields of sky. Sharp winds rise and leave as fast, and in a huff. Shapes shimmer through mists. Wet insinuates, a mix of fresh and salt. It is a place of change where eyes are tricked, distances lengthened.

Before there were standing stones at Stenness and Brodgar there were circles in the rock face, cut by farmers long ago with tools made of

other stones. So much effort to cut stone with stone – ditches deep and
wide – must have been driven by a determination to set the defined circle apart, to make it stand out as a special, even sacred, space; a clearing
in the forest after all the trees were gone. That need was met first of all
at Stenness. Stenness, so far as we know, is the oldest henge in the British Isles. In olden times the rock-cut ditch, scraped clean of soil and
grass, may have flooded from time to time and held water like a moat.
This would have made the interior space an island within the island of
Orkney: Mainland in miniature. Stepping into the circle would have
been another journey over water. They say Orcadians are farmers who
fish; Shetlanders on the archipelago beyond are fishermen who farm.
Both are caught between land and sea.

Fårö Island, off the northern tip of Gotland in the Baltic Sea, is a
place misunderstood even by modern-day Swedes. The name is older
than the Swedish most Swedes speak. It is Gutnish, a language with
Norse roots deeper than Vikings. In Gutnish, Fårö means 'the island
that must be travelled to'. Fårö is so close to Gotland it feels like somewhere you might swim to if need be. Ferries take cars there in minutes.
Hydrographers suggest the Baltic Sea might best be understood as the
estuary of the rivers that empty into it from surrounding lands. Its
waters were deeper in the distant past and as a consequence in the
Bronze Age, 3,000 to 4,000 years ago, Fårö would have been smaller
and further off, more of it submerged until a mere dot of land amid
the sea.

During the Bronze Age the ancestors of the Swedes, and of the
Vikings too, were in the habit of planting upright stones to make the
outlines of ships. Called 'ship settings' by archaeologists, they prolif-
erate on Gotland in particular. Made of stone and landlocked, you
might say they are the antithesis of anything that floats. But long
before the Vikings set sail in their longships, it seems their forefa-
thers were already in thrall to sea voyages, and making monuments

143

of them. As well as rendering hulls in stone they took to carving ships into the bedrock. Some of the best artworks of that sort are on Fårö.

I visited them one wintry day in 2012 with archaeologist Joakim Wehlin. The carvings were under ice, made from a recent flood of clean water, offering a lid thick enough to walk upon. The distance separating us from whoever had taken the time and made the effort to engrave the lines (a distance made of time) was made greater still by having to view his work through nature's lens. Hard to see, easily overlooked altogether, the etchings were spare of line, more reminiscent of insects with many legs. Ships they were though, apparently, with crews of oarsmen shown only by vertical lines.

We were well inland but Joakim deduced our location would have been coastal in the artist's day, overlooking the sea.

'This would have been a perfect place to meet,' he said, 'to discuss important things.'

He told me it would have taken effort to cross to Fårö in the Bronze Age, and some skill. Perhaps it was the journey that mattered; the setting aside of time; people absenting themselves from home to attend meetings, parliaments; gathering to declare war or negotiate peace; to share news of discoveries and innovations that might better the lives of all. There was a time of quests; journeys people made to prove themselves. Since their coming to Fårö depended on boats, possessions of great value in themselves, it seemingly mattered to mark all the effort, to memorialize it in stone. Joakim had me picture people gathering on that little island, pulling their various craft up beaches beyond the reach of the tide. Fårö may have been neutral territory where special rules and customs applied, and people felt safe.

In any event, some people are called to places on the edge. The same urge has taken our species into the air, into space, to the moon.

In the twenty-first century it is straightforward to travel to the opposite side of our planet in a single day. But a quest does not have to

144

cover thousands of miles to have meaning, to be life-changing. By our casual crossing of the Earth, even reaching into space, we may have diminished the meaning of other journeys. Crossing to Fårö, as to Orkney, is on a human scale: the destination visible from the point of departure. Viewed from the right angle such a journey might still be invested with meaning, like stepping over a ribbon of water made blue or grey by reflected sky and into a different place entirely.

Battersea Shield
and reaching for perfection

Then, round the very rim of the superbly
constructed shield, he placed the mighty
Stream of Ocean.

— HOMER,
The Iliad

E VERY WORD, EVERY name has meaning in its own right; every
one a story.

By the middle of the nineteenth century, London north of the
Thames was choked and filthy with humanity. Sculpted parkland on
the south bank, the newly created Battersea Park, promised space and
fresh air, so in the 1850s the two areas were connected. First called Victoria Bridge (a partner for nearby Albert), the span was renamed in
the 1860s after concerns were raised it might be structurally unsound.
Since any mishap or accident would have been linked with Her Majesty's name, Chelsea was superimposed as a neutral alternative. In the
end the thing was demolished and replaced with the present Chelsea
Bridge, in the years just before the outbreak of the Second World War.

Beneath the modern trappings lies an ancient truth more interesting. The bridges were built over a much older crossing point, in all

likelihood the ford by which Julius Caesar crossed the Thames in 54 BC. The place that would be London lay close to the junction of trackways, thoroughfares older than memory and threading east, west and north. There were two little hills north of the river (remembered as Ludgate and Cornhill) providing panoramic views all about. As well as the Thames, there were other waterways, the now subterranean Fleet and Walbrook, deep enough for ships. The land was fertile and had been worked by Neolithic farmers, prowled by Mesolithic hunters. There had been mammoths in Ilford, hippos in Brentford and rhinos where judges now sit bewigged in the courtrooms of the Old Bailey.

By the time of Caesar's arrival there was already a sophisticated Iron Age civilization in these islands. In Gaul, Germania and elsewhere on the continental mainland, Caesar had encountered those he knew as Celts, a word and a name adapted from the Greek *keltoi* meaning 'foreigner', 'not us'. Those iron men he met on this side of the water were of a similar sort, also bellicose and practised in the use of swords and knives like the Gauls, but with customs and ways distinct enough to earn them a different name. In answer to the Roman's question 'What is this place?' the locals apparently answered something like 'Pretani' or 'Britanni' (a tinkling, tinny sound, in a land rich in tin). 'Britannia' was the Roman's best attempt at repeating the name, and those who lived here, the natives, were therefore Britons.

That crossing point on the Thames was important in the minds of those Britons. As a name, 'Thames' winds and swirls all the way back to the Sanskrit *tamasa*, meaning 'dark water' (the Tamar that splits Cornwall from Devon has the same root). The peoples who first walked and then rowed or sailed into these islands came mostly from the east, bringing with them eastern languages. Everything we know – in the familiar landscape, in the words – is laid in layers, one on top of another, old over older. Tamasa . . . Tamyse . . . Tems . . . Thames . . . Its waters were made a final resting place for precious things – weapons and jewellery sacrificed in the hope of kindness or reward from benevolent gods and goddesses.

The Victorian workmen toiling on that first Chelsea Bridge found in the mud a bronze shield that had lain there for more than 2,000 years. Known as the Battersea Shield, it is more accurately described as a highly decorated covering for a shield likely made of wood or some other organic matter that did not survive. It measures two and a half feet tall by just over a foot wide and is regarded as a high-water mark of Iron Age art. Several pieces of bronze, beaten thin, were fastened together into one, using bronze rivets. Those joints were cleverly concealed beneath three raised circles – 'roundels' – filled with swirling decorations achieved with the repoussé technique of hammering a design into the back of sheet-metal until it protrudes from the front. The larger, central roundel has as its centrepiece a pronounced, domed boss the size of a clenched fist, behind which the shield's handle would have been secured. Within the roundels are twenty-seven buttons called enamel but which are actually made of opaque red glass given the appearance of droplets of blood. The decoration is in the style art historians label La Tène, after other treasures recovered from the shallows of Lake Neuchâtel in Switzerland, in the same year as the Battersea Shield was found. Some of the interlocking S-shapes in the roundels have been seen as variations on the theme of the swastika, an ancient eastern symbol of good fortune. Swastikas came out of the east too. *Swastika* is Sanskrit for wellbeing.

The Battersea Shield – so unique that art experts struggle to date it by comparison to anything else – is thought to have been made some time in the second century BC. As well as being influenced by a style it is ultimately a work of individual genius, untrammelled and free to find its own expression. It shows no signs of having been used in any fight and was, in all likelihood, made only as a votive offering by a warlord intent on giving thanks, or else asking for help. Archaeologists have imagined a chief or a king commissioning the piece from master craftsmen, perhaps soon after some or other triumph, or in the face of disaster, or tragedy. With ceremony and pomp he led his followers to the river and there surrendered the shield, bright as the sun, to dark water.

A shield might be more than something to stand behind. A shield might also tell a story. In Homer's *Iliad*, the goddess Thetis asks Hephaestus, lame blacksmith of the gods, to make a new shield for her son Achilles. Half god himself, Achilles had loaned his shield and armour to his dearest friend Patroclus. When Patroclus was killed in combat with Hector, Troy's greatest warrior, the armour was lost to the horse-taming Trojans. Achilles had been sitting out the battle, sulking about a personal slight from his leader Agamemnon. The death of Patroclus goaded him back into the fight however and, before he set out, his goddess mother, fearing for his life in the face of a warrior like Hector, sought special protection for him. Just a few lines of the *Iliad* describe Achilles' new body armour, 'brighter than blazing fire', a helmet topped with a gold crest, shin guards of soft tin. Four pages, however, are given to detailing his new shield, which has on it a depiction of all life: earth, sea and sky; sun and moon; the constellations; weddings and feasts; a family quarrel presided over by lawyers; war, siege and ambush; a field ploughed and a harvest reaped; vines heavy with grapes; a herd of heifers and a bull attacked by lions; a flock of sheep; men and women dancing; and around the shield's rim, encircling and encompassing all, the world's ocean. The shield, the description of it at least, was a message; an otherwise blank page filled from edge to edge with details. A message in a bottle; a reaching out in the hope of communicating to the future all that mattered then.

We can choose what sort of stories to tell. There has always been a place and a taste for dystopian visions – the worst that might happen. In interesting times, troubled times, the worst of times might preoccupy the imagination. The English poet W. H. Auden was preoccupied for a while with the Cold War between the USA and the communist countries of the Soviet Bloc. In 1952, when he wrote *The Shield of Achilles*, both sides kept planes in the air over central Europe all day and all night, loaded with atomic bombs, each ready to obliterate the other. The Korean War – a proxy for the mutual loathing of the west and the Soviets – was pounding away. Auden imagined a different context for Hephaestus as he worked on the shield. Instead of weddings and feasts, he saw a deathly land and countless people waiting there without hope; a disembodied voice droned a justification for the sterility; rather than peaceful cows he saw three figures bound to stakes, their spirits broken; instead of dancers he saw a barren field, a boy throwing stones at a bird, girls raped and two boys stabbing a third with a knife. Telling stories is what we do in an effort to make sense of existence and of our place within it – reaching out to whoever might hear and understand.

If there ever was a war waged by Greeks against the people of Troy – and historians cannot agree – then it was a thousand years and more BC. Homer, writing around 700 BC, wanted to give his audience a vision of a gilded past when god-like heroes rode into battle on chariots and fought duels with spears while women waited, fearing for their children.

The artists who created the Battersea Shield worked in a world still in thrall to gods and goddesses. With their skill, they spun a story of their own, written in flowing shapes and wine-dark stones. It is a story we cannot read, and yet in spite of our incomprehension we are still moved by the art of it. The story told by the Battersea Shield, that part we can intuit if not read, is also about striving, reaching. From the beginning, those makers understood their creation was destined for another world, that its time on their Earth would be short. With that in mind they reached beyond their own space and time, dispatching a message forward into the future. They understood too that they had borrowed their lifetimes as well as the bronze and the glass. In spite of that – or perhaps because of it – they expended every last ounce of effort in pursuit of perfection.

The RAF motto 'Per ardua ad astra' – through endeavour to the stars – is still familiar. It was coined by pilots at the time of the Great War, pilots with a classical education. In part the phrase has its roots in lines written by the Roman philosopher Seneca the Younger, in *Hercules Furens* ('The Mad Hercules'): 'non est ad astra mollis e terris via' – there is no easy way from Earth to the stars.

In accepting the need for hard work in order to make dreams real, there is implicit the notion that it is worth going further than necessary. The lesson of the Battersea Shield might be that reaching for perfection is always right, always best, regardless. Be better than you need to be.

8.

Heroes

Kirkburn Warrior
and the way of iron

Iron sharpeneth iron; so a man sharpeneth the
countenance of his friend.

— PROVERBS 27:17

I N 1987, AT Kirkburn in Yorkshire, archaeologists excavated an
Iron Age cemetery. In one grave they found the skeleton of a man
who died when he was somewhere between twenty and thirty-five
years old. Given that his fellows laid him down as long ago as the last
third of the first millennium BC, it is hard to be more precise about his
age. He lay on his left side, curled like a newborn baby, knees to his
chest. With him was a sword of iron, still in its scabbard and described
by specialists as the finest of its sort in all of Europe. It was a composite
item, made of seventy individual pieces brought together by a crafts-
man of great skill. The sword's hilt alone was made of thirty-seven
pieces of iron, horn and bronze. As well as being functional – and there
was evidence the sword had been broken at least once and repaired – it
was also highly decorative: scrolls and curls inscribed into the metal;
droplets of red glass fixed to the handle evoking blood freshly spilled.

Of all the elements in the universe, iron is the most stable. It is

155

number 26 on the Periodic Table of elements laid out in 1869 by Russian chemist Dmitri Ivanovich Mendeleev. He had noticed that certain properties of elements recurred periodically depending on how he organized them – or rather subject to the way nature organized them. He was so clever he left spaces in his table plan for elements unknown, to him and to his time, but whose existence and natures he could predict. Subsequent discoveries proved him right, and filled in the gaps. We know of 118 elements so far. Of those, a hundred are the product of dying stars; the rest occur in nuclear reactors or in consequence of choreographed collisions in particle accelerators such as the Large Hadron Collider in Switzerland.

Elements are made of atoms, specks imagined by Ancient Greeks as the smallest of the small. We have since learned that atoms are a long way from being smallest. An atom, such as we visualize it, is, like the universe, mostly empty space. At its centre the nucleus is orbited, like a teensy planet, by one or more smaller electrons. Every nucleus of every atom is made of smaller specks called neutrons and protons, and the number of protons gives the atomic number of the element. The nucleus of an iron atom has precisely 26 protons and so the atomic number of iron is 26; on the Periodic Table iron occupies place 26. Simple and orderly. In all the universe, the relationship between iron's protons and neutrons is uniquely harmonious. If they were guests around a dinner table they would be chatting and enjoying the food. The nuclei of other elements are not like that. Those of heavy elements such as polonium and uranium have so many protons they are unstable, raucous and agitated. In their case you might say there are not enough seats around the dinner table so the element seeks to shed protons, unwanted guests, and have them go elsewhere. This discarding of protons is seen by us, described by us, as radioactivity. Lighter elements such as hydrogen and helium have the opposite problem. At their dinner parties, the atmosphere would be relaxed if only there were more protons to go around. As it is, all the empty seats make for another kind of upset and discord.

Iron is therefore unique among the elements. While the hearts of all the others are places of storms without end, that of iron knows Zen-like balance and calm. Like the porridge Goldilocks prefers, iron is just right. All the other elements might wish they were like iron but they are not.

It took our species a long time to discover the metal iron makes. Just as the farmers of Callanish could not have known the Lewisian gneiss they built with was some of the oldest rock on Earth, so the first blacksmiths could only have been oblivious to iron's elemental calm. Copper and gold were fancied first, since they are pretty and appear on Earth's surface as nuggets, Easter eggs for the finding. Malleable enough, like frozen butter, they could be hammered into shape just as they were. By some experimenting genius, copper was brought together in a crucible with silvery tin – an arranged marriage made at 1,100°C – to create the alloy bronze. Bronze is glamorous too. Newly cooked bronze is golden as sunlight with the shine of liquid honey. To watch a smith pour molten bronze into a clay mould and, seconds later, pull from it a golden sword (a sword from a stone) is as close to Merlin's magic as a mortal might need to get. Anyone and everyone in their right mind wants bronze, loves bronze. For thousands of years it was bronze the ancient world coveted. Hector's sword was bronze, so too that of Achilles and all the brittle heroes who inspired Homer's prose.

Iron is a plain-Jane, and ornery to boot. Plain, yet she plays hard to get. Iron demands 1,500 degrees of heat in which to melt and run, the temperature of a blast furnace. At first and for the longest time such a temperature was out of reach of humankind. The first smiths had only poor clay and fires and so it was as much as they could do to coax powdered iron ore into sullen clumps, grey-black misshapen broccoli heads they called bloom. Bloom demanded heating a second time in a fire boosted by bellows until the softened mass might be beaten on the anvil with the hammer. In this way the liquefied slag was driven out, like snot, until wrought iron was the result. Wrought iron, hard won and hard to love for its looks alone, might then be thinking itself tortured in the fire but the tempered blade looking back and knowing better.

Bronze is brittle and unbending, apt to snap. Dull iron has give and so flexes and forgives the clumsy knock of ploughshare on buried sarsen, the murderous strike of sword on sword. A broken iron sickle was easily mended by the smith, a blunted iron blade readily resharpened. Man forged iron and so iron forged mankind, taught us to better ourselves through endeavour and striving. Those first smiths could not have known about iron's quiet heart but they came to understand the stuff they could make was sound and strong and stable and they never looked back. No metal has mattered more in the building of us.

Iron were the swords of the Romans who splashed ashore on the south-east of the long island in AD 43. To me, the Romans were as dull as the stuff of their blades – bringers of taxation, straight roads and uniforms for dreary jobs with dreary names. Bureaucrats and desk-jockeys the lot of them. We think as highly of them as we do because we recognize our world in theirs. They seem modern and so we hold them in high regard. In these islands, as elsewhere, the Romans encountered natives armed with iron weapons. For several hundred years before the Claudian invasion, the technology of iron was known here too. Before the Romans unloaded their cargo of civilization the people living here already had an idiosyncratic understanding of what it meant to be alive. They had come to iron by themselves and were already the better for it.

Before the social revolution wrought by Rome, the natives had been through a great disruption of their own. For a thousand years the glittery bronze had held them in its thrall. Access to bronze often meant forging and maintaining connections with those people who controlled scarce raw materials in distant lands. A taut web of relationships gave society a definite, unyielding shape. Status was conferred on those who had the tin mines, the copper mines. Power was based upon control of the movement of those ingredients and of the finished items. During the millennium before the birth of Christ, for reasons still not understood, bronze lost its allure. Archaeologists have offered all sorts of explanations: a collapse of confidence in the commodity, or overproduction leading to a glut that crashed its price. Most plausible is the suggestion that those who had always been left powerless by their inability to have and control the bronze finally turned their backs on it completely. Instead they struck out in a new direction and took society with them. Those who had been forever sidelined and overlooked by the world of bronze sought to forge new connections, make new bonds. Instead of looking beyond the horizon for the stuff of power, they united with their own neighbours and found power beneath their feet in their own fields. They forged bonds with those around them, close at hand.

The grave at Kirkburn is the power and the lesson of iron made manifest. Here was a man, a warrior. Most intriguing of all, awe-inspiring, careful excavation revealed that before it was backfilled, three spears were thrust into his grave. The archaeologists could not say for certain but the points may have deliberately pierced the body. Only then was he covered over, and whatever mound was raised above him, the shafts were left protruding from it. Who can say precisely what the act meant to those who performed it? Perhaps he was a fighting man, a brave man who died in his bed, denied a warrior's death. Did his fellows seek to make amends by inflicting deadly wounds post-mortem? In any event his prickled grave would have been conspicuous, for all to see and wonder at.

The way of the warrior was simple like iron, steadfast and trustworthy. The warrior armed with the iron tools of his trade defined a simple shape that was easily read by all. The way of the warrior was hardly a life for everyone, for every man, but it was clear to see – a straight, clear path to follow or not. Not everyone chooses to walk the line but it is vital to know where the line is. Iron was the foundation for communities, people making the most of their neighbours and the resources closest to hand. Like flawed humanity, iron demanded effort and perseverance if the best results were to be obtained. We have been at our best as small communities pulling together. Generations of steady effort by individuals committed to their own patch and to each other have been the foundation of the greatest success, the greatest achievements. The philanthropist-industrialist Andrew Carnegie said most people tended to overlook opportunity 'because it comes wearing overalls and looks like hard work'. So it is with iron, and its lesson is that hard work and community are the basis for all that has been good in society.

Whakatane

and the courage required to
do what must be done

Taia o moko, hai hoa matenga mou. You may lose
your most valuable property through misfortune in
various ways . . . you may be robbed of all your most
prized possessions, but of your moko you cannot be
deprived. Except by death. It will be your ornament
and your companion until your last day.

– JAMES COWAN,
'Maori tattooing survivals – some notes on moko'
in *Journal of the Polynesian Society* 30 (1921)

POLYNESIANS BEGAN EXPLORING the Pacific Ocean and colo-
nizing its islands from around 3,000 years ago. Across seemingly
trackless oceans, they navigated a triangle of seascape stretched
between Hawaii in the north, Easter Island in the east and New Zealand in the west. Their journeys were not one-way odysseys, trusting in
luck and settling wherever they made landfall, but planned return trips
made by mariners confident of their skills and able to tell where they
were at any time.

Aboard each vessel was a navigator, responsible for paying attention to and remembering every moment of the journey. These way-finders were trained from infancy, first of all placed in the shallows of the sea to feel and remember the pull and push of the tide. They practised 'dead reckoning', where position *now* is determined by knowing where one has *been*. Each navigator maintained a meditative state for hours and days on end, noticing and allowing for every change of wind, every ocean current, every variation in speed. From the rhythm of waves striking the hull, the way-finder would identify the fingerprints, or rather waveprints, impressed into the passing water by islands and archipelagos many miles away. By reading the patterns on the ocean's surface, the way-finder might pull the desired island out of the ocean beyond, winding it towards the vessel's bow as though it were attached by an invisible string. By night, he watched the wanderings of stars and planets and imagined it was the vessel and the world that stayed in place while the cosmos moved about them.

When European sailors found Polynesian voyagers all over the Pacific, scattered across tens of millions of square miles of ocean, they preferred to imagine those natives had been blown there by chance – survivors tossed at the whim of the sea. Only as the years went by did they begin to appreciate the sophistication of mariners who thought and felt their way over the waves, across the unblinking eye of the world's largest ocean.

This was the world before writing, before maps and charts. This was the world of memory, where necessary things were those that people carried squirrelled inside their heads. Socrates opposed the practice of writing. In Plato's *Phaedrus* he noted: 'For this invention will produce forgetfulness in the minds of those who learn to use it, because they will not practise their memory . . . You have invented an elixir not of memory but of reminding; and you offer your pupils the appearance of wisdom but not true wisdom.' This was the world where each individual took responsibility for remembering and knowing some part of the whole; a world in which every contribution from every soul was vital to the wellbeing of the group.

The folklore of the Maori is rich with memories of great voyages. Kupe is revered by many clans as the first to find his way from the mythical Maori home island of Hawaiki to Aotearoa, the land of the long white cloud, known to the English-speaking world as New Zealand. According to the legend, he noticed the species of birds they called *kuaka* flying south at the same time every year. Never were the birds seen to land, so Kupe and his ilk questioned, 'Kua kite te koanga kuaka? Ko wai ka kite I te hua o te kuaka?' ('Who has seen the nest of the kuaka? Who has ever held the egg of the kuaka?')*

Persuaded by the notion of land out there to the south – the kuaka's destination – he set sail with a small team and followed where they went. So numerous were the birds in the sky that they reminded him of chips of wood flying from the adzes of men carving canoes from tree trunks. By night, the birds' calls were so loud that Kupe could follow their sound in the darkness.

Inspired and emboldened, Kupe kept faith with the kuaka and so made it with his followers all the way to Aotearoa – as long ago as 1200 BC, if the clans have it right. Thereafter his people back on Hawaiki (a place that exists now only as part of the Maori sense of heaven itself) were able to follow where he had led, and so to colonize the new land that was to be their home ever after.

Some time around 1000 BC, a great double-hulled canoe with scores of men and women aboard arrived in the Bay of Plenty on the north-east coast of the North Island. The huge *Mataatua waka* (*waka* means 'canoe') had travelled from Hawaiki in the north in search of fresh supplies of sweet potato. A chief called Toroa was in command of

---

* *Kuaka* is Maori for the godwit, masters of marathon flight. Adult birds fly non-stop from the Arctic to New Zealand every year, a journey of 8,000 miles in one go. It is an unequalled feat. In the weeks before departure they eat until they nearly double their size. Internal organs not needed for flight are all but cut off from blood supplies and so shrink; the extra blood is diverted to their wings to power the nine-day flight.

the voyage, and he and the rest of the men left the vessel behind in the shallows and splashed ashore. While they were gone, the canoe began to drift out of the bay, like a seabird on the back of the receding tide. The women and children left aboard were afraid they would be pulled into deep water where the waves might capsize the vessel. They were made helpless by the fact it was forbidden by law for women to touch the paddles of the *waka*, far less use them to power the vessel. All seemed lost until one young woman spoke up and acted as she saw fit. She was Princess Wairaka, daughter of Toroa. Unafraid, she grabbed one of the paddles, leapt on to one of the *waka*'s outriggers and began paddling powerfully.

'Kia whakatane au I ahua!' she shouted. 'I will do what a man does!'

Emboldened by her actions, more of the women joined her in the effort and all were saved.

Whaka is the Maori verb 'to do'; *tane* is 'male' or 'man'. A town on the Bay of Plenty is called Whakatane in honour of Wairaka's defiant bravery. Out on a clenched fist of rock in the river flowing into the sea is a bronze statue of her, tall and ethereal as an elf.

Like every other indigenous population engulfed by Europeans, the Maori suffered injustices and cruelty at the hands of the incomers. The French, prowling too, seemed more blatantly acquisitive, ready to seize what they wanted by force alone. By signing the Treaty of Waitangi with Queen Victoria's British Empire in 1840, the Maori believed their lands would not be taken from them without consent, or at least a bill of sale. It was not to be so simple however. War with the British followed five years later and dragged on for several decades. Hostilities ended in 1872, and in the aftermath the Maori saw vast tracts of their territory confiscated by the British colonists in punitive acts of revenge. In spite of many attempts since at settlement and reconciliation, ill feeling hangs over the islands to this day.

The Maori lived in a world without metals and fought with weapons of wood and polished stone, but throughout the fighting proved to be among the most resilient and potent enemies Victoria's soldiers had faced anywhere in the world. Lessons the Maori taught those regiments about the effectiveness of guerrilla warfare and the use of trenches were not forgotten by the invaders and would be used by them in other parts of the world soon enough.

Proud defiance was graven deep in Maori souls; those the Europeans first encountered made indelible impressions. For one thing, the Maori were the most enthusiastic cannibals in the world. Inter-clan warfare was endemic and brutal. Prisoners taken in the aftermath of battles were routinely slaughtered and eaten. There was no greater victory, no greater humiliation to inflict, than transforming the vanquished into shit.

Sailors horrified by the eating of human flesh were especially impressed, however, by their tattoos. The word tattoo, so commonplace now, arrived in the west as a corruption of the Samoan *tatau*, meaning 'to strike'. Painted European folk like Celts, Gauls and Picts were long forgotten, so the fashion was reacquired from elsewhere. Rediscovered in the east, the designs fascinated the sailors who soon sought tattoos of their own. Among the Maori the practice was taken to an extreme, with whole faces as well as bodies permanently marked with wondrous swirling designs. Facial tattoos were called *ta-moko* and were made not with needles but with *uhi* – chisels shaped from albatross bones and used along with hammers to cut lines into the skin. Pigments made from caterpillar fungus, charcoal and kauri gum stained the wounds permanently dark. Botanist Joseph Banks accompanied Captain James Cook aboard HMS *Endeavour* and in 1769 made notes about the markings he saw among the Maori:

> Their faces are the most remarkable, on them they by some art unknown to me dig furrows in their faces a line deep at least and as broad, the edges of which are often indented and most perfectly black. This may be done to make them look frightful in war . . . Yet ugly as this certainly looks it is impossible to avoid

admiring the immense Elegance and Justness of the figures . . .
which in the face is always different spirals . . . all these finished
with a masterly taste and execution.

Central to *ta-moko*, as to all Maori art, is the *koru* that is their word
for a coil. This is present in the unfurling of a silver fern in springtime
and in the closing curl of a wave breaking on a beach. It is even there in
the corporate livery of Air New Zealand, the national carrier. The outside of the *koru* is new life and ceaseless movement, burgeoning potential
and growth; the inside maps the way back to the centre of all things, to
the infinite singularity that existed before the beginning of time.

Long ago the kuaka led the way to the land of the long white cloud.
Tiny yet indomitable in the face of enormity, through their determination they showed what was possible and proved any distance might be
traversed, any goal reached, any challenge met. Wairaka, founding force
of the place they now call Whakatane, was the daughter of a chief, a
princess, and therefore high-born. It is impossible to imagine she did
not bear the *moko* in her flesh; surely when she pushed the paddle deep,
pulled on it and thrust out her chin, it was cut with the *koru*, the looping
coil, the shape of the circle without end that has defined and driven the
destiny of our species. Wairaka made her memory immortal through
her actions. Raised in a world of confining traditions and rules, she
understood the need to be defiant when necessary, to act regardless of
the risk of censure or punishment, for the sake of the greater good. She
did what had to be done, and damn the consequences. Too often today
we find ourselves herded into groups, our behaviour governed by group-
think. Now as never before we should remember we are individuals first
and always – unique, each of us a singularity. Each of us has the power
and, more than that, the absolute responsibility to act for the greater
good. With every thought and move we can make the universe itself
slightly worse or slightly better. Any failure to do the latter is down to
each individual. The buck stops with each one of us.

Y Gododdin
and a special kind of noticing

One remembers with special vividness too
because military training is very largely training
in alertness and a special kind of noticing.

— PAUL FUSSELL,
The Great War and Modern Memory

AMERICAN WRITER Paul Fussell served as an officer in the
Second World War, winning the Purple Heart and Bronze Star
while fighting in France. In *The Great War and Modern Memory* he
wrote about how a simmering, ever-present fear of death served to
intensify the soldierly experience, imbuing everyday moments and
objects with seeming significance, 'trivial things like single poppies or
the scars on a rifle stock . . . When a man imagines that every moment
is his next to last, he observes and treasures up sensory details purely for
their own sake.' War sharpens the senses, makes a person pay attention
to details and so remember them with a unique acuity – a special kind
of noticing.

More than a century has passed since the ending of the First World
War. The last of its veterans are dead and the events are beyond the
reach of living memory, pushed over the sill into history. We might

imagine a hundred years is long enough for forgetting and for recovery, that the hurt is all behind us. Both of my grandfathers fought in that war. I know precious little of their experiences. Both were wounded (my mum's dad, James, in Gallipoli, while still a teenager, my dad's dad, Robert, in France) and both survived. I have wondered about the uncountable, unknowable details of all soldiers' lives. The First World War killed 20 million people and injured 20 million more. What kind of special noticing would be required to know the details, the minutiae, of all those lives, to remember them properly and keep them safe? How much is remembered now, how much is forgotten?

It feels unforgivably banal to say that the events of 1914 to 1918 changed everything. But that simple truth bears remembering. That war has been described as a set of iron railings separating the past from the present. It is possible to see through those railings, but on account of the immovable barrier they present we can never properly know, far less touch, that past again.

'Out of the world of summer, 1914, marched a unique generation,' wrote Fussell.

Those soldiers left behind a Britain that had not known an engulf- ing war for most of a century – not since Napoleon had cast his shadow over Europe, when their predecessors had worn red tunics with shin- ing brass buttons, or rode on horseback with sabres at their sides. What followed that summer of 1914 was made all the more obscene and despoiling by the intense memories of seemingly unadulterated perfec- tion. 'One read outdoors, went on picnics, had tea served from a white wicker table under the trees,' wrote Fussell. 'You could leave your books on the table all night without fear of rain.' The naivety of such words, redolent not just of a social class but of a time untainted by the century to come, is enough to make a reader wince. Irony was one of the prod- ucts of the First World War and we see it plainly in the innocent, trusting enjoyment of that last summer, while the enveloping horror that was to come waited just beyond the horizon.

It has only been a hundred years. Between 1939 and 1945 the peoples of the world did it all again. Some historians view the two wars as all of a piece, seeing 1914 to 1945 as a second Thirty Years War. It was the most unspeakable, unforgiven horror our species has inflicted upon itself so far. It is a mistake to imagine we are remotely close to being beyond it. We are the hopelessly damaged children of a hopelessly damaged family and all the messes we live among now are the direct or indirect consequences of what happened to those elders. It has only been a hundred years and already there are adult generations alive who do not even know how much they do not know about what happened, and why. This absence frightens me.

Y Gododdin is a long poem about people long ago. It was written some time between AD 600 and 1200 and records a battle fought around the year 600 between Britons and Angles, somewhere in the north of England. (So vague, but remembering is hard, a constant fight.) A near-legendary Welsh scribe or bard called Aneirin is generally credited as the author but most of the details are uncertain now.

It tells the tale of the Gododdin, who were the tribe known to the Romans as the Votadini. They had controlled a swatch of territory straddling parts of southern Scotland and northern England, and when the Romans withdrew in the 400s, the power vacuum pulled Angles, a Germanic people from northern Europe, across the North Sea, a grey stretch of water they called the Gannet's Bath. Whether they came to conquer, to colonize or just to try their luck is among much else that historians argue about concerning the time we used to call the Dark Ages. Soon they were present in the territory that would be known as Northumbria. In a bid to turn back the tide overwhelming his tribal lands, Mynyddog Mwynfawr, leader of the Gododdin, proposed an alliance with other Brythonic kingdoms to his west and south.

According to the poem, the resultant rainbow alliance of warriors gathered at the capital of the Gododdin, called Din Eidyn – the place we know as Edinburgh. For a year, Mynyddog was host to them. The poem tells of 300 fighting men fed and watered and given gifts for all of that time, readying themselves for what lay ahead. Finally they rode out of Din Eidyn and made their way to a place called Catraeth, usually understood as Catterick in North Yorkshire. According to the poem, the Brythonic army was massively outnumbered:

> Men went to Catraeth with the dawn;
> Their fears left them.
> A hundred thousand and three hundred clashed together;
> They stained their spears, splashed with blood.
> He was at the forefront, foremost in battle,
> Before the retinue of Mynyddog Mwynfawr.

In spite of the overwhelming odds, all fought bravely until only one man of the Gododdin was left to tell the tale.

> Three hundred gold-torqued men attacked;
> Guarding their land, bloody was the slaughter.
> Although they were slain, they slew,
> And until the end of the world they will be honoured
> And of all of us kinsmen who went together
> Sad, but for one man, none escaped.

Y Gododdin is not history in any conventional sense; rather the verses of the poem are lamentations for the warriors killed in the fight. It is stirring stuff – a proud telling of selfless deeds and clear-eyed bravery. Individual warriors are named, singled out for their acts of valour.

One of those, a description of a Gododdin man named Gwawrddur, may provide the earliest written reference to King Arthur:

> He charged before three hundred of the finest;
> He cut down both centre and wing;
> He excelled in the forefront of the noblest host;
> He gave gifts of horses from the herd in winter;
> He fed black ravens on the rampart of a fortress.
> Though he was no Arthur
> Among the powerful ones in battle
> In the front rank, a palisade was Gwawrddur.

On and on it goes, a tale of brotherhood and valour. It is easy to be carried away by the rhythm and cadence, to feel the hackles rise. What is surely hidden though, left unrecorded, is a host of other men, forgotten men. That Mynyddog took only 300 to fight a force of thousands is untenable. Whatever else was planned for the place called Catraeth, it seems safe to assume it was no deliberate mass suicide. In the train of the 300 must have marched a host of others, foot soldiers whose lives were every bit as dear to them and theirs. But whoever wrote the poem, Aneirin or some other, saw no reason even to mention them. *Y Gododdin* recounts only what happened to 300 men of the highest rank – great men of their time. What is left out, deemed unworthy of so much as a mention, is the life and death of an entire army. More than 1,400 years have passed since the conflict in question and the common men who fell are forgotten, as though they had never been. Only a hundred years have passed since the First World War and already the process of forgetting millions is well underway. It is subtle, insidious, and has been at work from the beginning, even while the bullets and shells were still in the air alongside the larks.

Before the Battle of the Somme, a British soldier wore just one dog tag. If he died then it was taken from around his neck to ensure his pay

172

was stopped (the British Army does not pay wages to dead soldiers). The system worked well enough, until the opening of the great charnel houses in which so many died together that it was easy to lose track of names. After the first few days of the Somme, tens of thousands of dog tags had been taken from tens of thousands of corpses, or bits of corpses. Others had flown through the air from men transformed by monstrous explosions and shredding shrapnel into nothing but clouds of crimson mist that were borne away on the wind. When the time came to bury all that butchered meat, no one was sure any longer what was what and who was who. The Army bureaucrats knew who was dead – the bundled dog tags told them that much – but each man and boy had been permanently separated from his name. The serried ranks of Portland stone in the graveyards of the Western Front suggest there is a man beneath each, neatly laid. In reality they were often mass graves, the dead heaped hurriedly together. Only later, in the quiet of a sullen peace, were stones set in place in columns and rows and grass sown, weaving an illusion of order over unspeakable chaos beneath. After the Somme, the lesson learned, each fighting man was issued with two tags – one that might stop his pay in the event of his death and the other left around his neck, if he had one, so he might at least be buried with his name.

It was too late for many. The looming brick and stone memorial at Thiepval in northern France remembers the Missing of the Somme, the 72,337 (and counting – more bodies are being unearthed by farmers year on year) who died thereabouts and yet have no known grave. Many have 'no known grave' only because they were separated from their names.

All too soon the terrifying numbers of dead were being eulogized – by news reporters, poets, authors – as 'the fallen'. Still within the reach of living memory, the hundreds of thousands became a combined entity, a community of death within which individual identities were swallowed. They grew not old, as those that remembered them grew old right enough. And having aged, those who had remembered them – their faces, voices, characters, their hopes and dreams – died too in their time. The dead of the First World War, and the Second – the missing, the fallen – are drifting out of reach. Soon they will be no more than names on stones, stories in books.

It is 1,400 years since Catraeth and all but a handful of the dead Gododdin are utterly forgotten now, as lost to legend as Hector and Achilles. Plaque after plaque promises that the names of the world war casualties live for evermore, but they will not, they cannot. Those who took part in those twentieth-century bloodbaths might as well have died at Troy, or Carthage, or Thermopylae . . . or Catraeth. We will not remember them, not in any way that matters. We will not remember, as their parents did, their first faltering steps. We will not remember why their sweethearts loved them; which books were their favourites; what jokes made them laugh; how they parted their hair.

We are, or should be at the very least, at war with the forgetting. Maybe it is a fight we cannot win, but still it matters to fight the darkness. The warning of *Y Gododdin* is that all shall be forgotten.

But we are living in a wounded world – war-wounded. Those injured by war are still among us and always will be because war never stops and the casualties keep coming home. Most of the wounds are invisible to the eye, but each surviving veteran is a living reminder of what war does. The world as it is today is one still recovering from all the hurt of those terrible thirty years of the century just past. Call it shell shock like they used to, or combat stress, or post-traumatic stress disorder. Our civilizations are walking wounded, and the simmering aggressions between the nations of today are the glowing embers left behind by the First and Second World Wars. To think we are over it all, beyond it, is a gross and dangerous mistake. Even now, with hot war raging in God-forsaken corners of the Earth, we imagine it cannot happen again to us. Seven decades of peace in western

Europe have lured us into thinking war is history for us here. But war is always waiting in the wings and we must remember what it does when it comes. We would do better to look for and see the wounds we bear, as individuals as well as nations. We could start by looking out for those freshly hurt and still living with the consequences. In this way we will remember the harm we have done, and that was done to us. See the wounds now, know them now, mark them with a special kind of noticing.

9.

Stories

Eden Whalers
and the Law of the Tongue

For that which befalleth the sons of men befalleth
beasts; even one thing befalleth them: as the one
dieth, so dieth the other; yea, they have all one
breath; so that a man hath no pre-eminence
above a beast: for all is vanity.

– ECCLESIASTES 3:19

W HEN I VISITED the Eden Killer Whale Museum in New South Wales, Australia, there was a scuba diver's suit on display in the entrance. I was there to learn about a local legend of a unique relationship between orcas and nineteenth-century whalers but my attention was held by the suit. Folded over the neoprene shoulders was a tabard of lead plate that covered front and back. The suit belonged to abalone fisherman Eric Nerhus and its weight had kept him on the seabed while he collected his wild harvest. My eye had been drawn by tooth marks in the lead, a necklace pattern of deep punctures, like a dotted line for tearing.

The accompanying label described how Eric had been collecting abalone alone on the seabed one day when suddenly all went dark and he was being shaken like a rag. A white pointer shark – better known as a great white – had attacked him directly from above, taking his head, shoulders and torso into its cavernous maw before biting down. Only the thick lead had prevented Eric from being bitten in two. He managed to get an arm free and stabbed at the beast's head and eye with the chisel he had been using to harvest the molluscs. After hellish seconds, the shark let go and withdrew into the depths. Eric's options were limited; with a broken nose, and bleeding from multiple wounds, he knew he had to surface and get help but was too deep to rise in one go. Rattled by the attack and by the knowledge the shark was likely nearby, still he had the presence of mind to rise only halfway on his weighted line before stopping and waiting, to allow the necessary decompression. While he dangled in the half dark, a tasty meal in a billowing cloud of his own blood, he watched the minute hand on his watch. Sufficient time having passed, Eric rose to the surface and, once back aboard his boat, to safety.

The suit serves as a reminder that the ocean is not our kingdom: other kings and queens reign there. In Eden they tell a story about orcas reaching out to men. Orca. Killer whale. Its scientific name is *Orcinus orca*. Orcinus is a Roman name for the god of the world below. *Orca* is Latin for a barrel – a reference to the round and bulky body of the beast. Spanish fishermen call them *ballena asesina*, which means 'assassin whale'. Orcas kill and eat other whales and dolphins, so more precise than the killer whale moniker is whale killer, for that is what they do.

Beneath the Pinturas Valley in the Santa Cruz province of Argentinian Patagonia there is a cavern called Cueva de las Manos – the Cave of the Hands. The name relates to artwork on the pale limestone walls, made when the world's temperature was slowly rising at the end of the last ice age, the climate growing kinder. People there and then, 10,000 and more years ago, were in the habit of using their hands as stencils – placing them palms down against the rock and blowing pigment or paint against the backs so that when they pulled their hands away they left spread-fingered prints. Waving from the cave walls are dozens, scores of raised hands. The effect is of looking at a classroom full of pupils vying for teacher's attention. We cannot know the reason why they did it, but perhaps some of the motivation was the desire to leave behind a personal mark: I was here. Whatever the inspiration, it was an act made possible by having hands.

On the ceiling of the Sistine Chapel in Rome, the Christian God and Adam reach their hands towards each other. This is the moment of the creation of humanity as imagined by Michelangelo. Their fingers do not touch; life must leap the gap like a spark, or a thought across a synapse.

Human hands have a long history. In the forests of 50 million years ago there were two kinds of mammal, both small like shrews. One sort opted to stay on the ground while the other climbed upwards. Those latter are, in the very vaguest sense, our ancestors. The little creatures that moved among the branches would in time give rise to the primates, and therefore us. Movement in the canopy posed obvious risks and those that did best, and had more offspring, adapted to cling and hold. Long digits became fingers. Most important of all in the long run, one of those digits became the opposable thumb that has made all the difference to the survival, and ultimately to the dominance, of our species.

Around the same time – 50 million or so years ago – mammals akin to hippos turned their backs on the land for the last time. Their preference for the water undid any need for hands, digits, fingers. Some of them gave rise, over millions of years of evolution, to creatures of great size – dolphins and whales. The biggest of them – blue whales and bow whales – are probably the largest living things Earth has known. The brains of the whales are large too, some much larger than our own. But whales and dolphins cannot interact with their three-dimensional world in the way we do with ours. They make no tools and cannot modify their environment. They have families, certainly; they care for one another and communicate among themselves; they hunt; but civilization is beyond them. They are observers of their world, not shapers or makers.

It was European settlers of New South Wales who named their fledgling town Eden in the early 1840s, after George Eden, 1st Earl of Auckland and British Secretary for the Colonies. Since 1828 there had been a whaling station there, taking advantage of the humpback whales that migrated up and down Australia's eastern seaboard. For at least 10,000 years before the settlers arrived, that part of the coast was home to people of the Thaua clan, of the Yuin nation. Like the white cuckoos in their nest, the Thaua were sometimes hunters of humpback whales. At first, the incomers took exception to the orcas that prowled around their boats, seeming to challenge them for access to the leviathans, and sought to fight them off, drive them away. Thaua men were employed on the whaling ships but they refused to hurt, far less kill, the orcas. Those were fellow hunters, they said, and would work alongside men in return for first choice of the meat of the humpbacks and other giants. What the orcas wanted were the huge tongues and lips. They would bring the humpbacks to the ships and prevent them escaping in return for their share. The Thaua called the deal the Law of the Tongue.

Despite the advice, most of the whites scorned the very idea. One family however, the Davidsons, saw the wisdom of the indigenous thinking. George Davidson was among the first generation of his family to set up as a whaler, establishing a station on Twofold Bay close by Eden town. He had been as sceptical as the rest at first, chasing off the orcas, but soon enough they began listening to the Thaua, and obeying the Law of the Tongue. By the middle of the nineteenth century they were among the most successful whalers in the area. The hulls of their ships were painted green and it was said the orcas knew them by sight. In the later months of each year the same pod of orcas would come to

Twofold Bay looking for food. One large male in particular would come close to the Davidson buildings on the shore, or to any green-hulled vessels, to attract their attention.

They called him Old Tom, and his antics became legend. Once his pod had shepherded some baleens in close he would swim into Twofold Bay, night or day, and begin breaching and slapping his great tail on the water until the Davidsons put to sea. Sometimes he was so keen to get the men into position with their harpoons he would grab the rope fixed to the lead boat and, holding it between his clamped teeth, drag the vessel towards the waiting whales. Always the Law was obeyed. The men would harpoon and kill the whales and then let Old Tom and his family help themselves. Like most orca pods, the real leader was female – a matriarch the men called Stranger who was aloof but in overall control. She ensured the pod never touched the flesh and blubber the men were after, so the deal was sweet for all. Sometimes a harpooned baleen would thrash and upset a rowing boat, casting the men into the water. Since the tradition was that whalers did not learn to swim, in order that they might have more respect for the sea, such accidents could be fatal. The orcas would intervene, keeping sharks away and the men afloat until they could be rescued. Sometimes men who had gone under were hauled or buoyed to the surface by the orcas. If ever an orca became trapped in ropes or nets, the men made sure to free them, and rescued orcas were heard purring their appreciation. It was a bond between men and beasts that lasted the best part of a century: three generations of the Davidson family maintained the relationship with Old Tom and Stranger and the rest.

When Old Tom finally died, his body was found washed up in Two-fold Bay. His skeleton is on display now in the Eden Killer Whale Museum, his teeth worn like belaying pins from gripping and hauling ropes.

All around the world there are indigenous people like the Thaua with bonds to orcas. Among the First Nations of North America the killers are regarded as reincarnations of the ancestors.

The Thaua's Law of the Tongue was based on an understanding by the orcas. They were more than capable of killing whales by themselves but it seems their kind had watched men at work, down through the millennia, and understood those creatures armed with sharp sticks were fellow hunters and uniquely skilled. According to the Thaua, the first approach for collaboration came not from men but from orcas. The cooperation was the whales' idea. They understood the nature of their handicap, their limitation, and so sought out those more able. Fifty million years after their ancestors had abandoned the land, still they felt the lack of hands and so came in search of those equipped with them.

Over in New Zealand in 2016 I visited Farewell Spit on the northern tip of South Island. A 16-mile-long sliver of sand, it has been a graveyard for pilot whales. Time and again whole pods come ashore there and, despite the efforts of well-meaning volunteers determined to refloat them, the animals usually die, often by the hundreds. It is a tragedy that has been happening for as long as there have been whales. A Maori elder I spoke to said it seemed the strandings were often led by a single sick animal. Since family ties within pods are unbreakable, the healthy members follow their sick relation into the shallows, even if it must ensure their doom. The elder said it seemed sick whales want to rest. They want to get on to the beach where they think they will be able to repose and breathe without also having to swim. It turns out sick whales just want to stop and lie down – and that all whales might lament the consequences of their ancestors' decision to choose lives of perpetual motion in the ocean.

We think we are so clever. Our species has risen to dominate all others. But it is our hands that have made all the difference. With our hands we have made all the tools, shaped all the technology. We have touched, held and seized whatever we have wanted. Without hands, none of our dreams would have been made real.

For all their majesty, their undoubted mastery of the ocean realm, the clever, thinking orcas still feel the lack of hands. Some of them sought a remedy at Eden by striking a partnership with handy humankind. The lesson of Eden and the orcas is the extent to which our destiny has been shaped by a decision made in the forests of 50 million years ago . . . by shrews.

Kerala Fire Ritual
and the sounds before words

To live at all is miracle enough.

— MERVYN PEAKE,
'To Live Is Miracle Enough'

I T HAD HARDLY been accomplished in one go; rather, it was a trek of thousands of miles by a thread of shadows strung out across time. The ancestors of the first Indians may have left the Horn of Africa 100,000 years ago, first crossing land and then water into the territory we know as Yemen. For millennia, the descendants of those emigrants traipsed towards the rising sun and then south down the western seaboard of the elephant's ear of India. Who can say how much, if anything, was remembered by then of their ancestors' African origins? Those wanderers who reached the tip of India became, in their turn, the ancestors of the modern inhabitants of the southernmost region of Kerala.

Between 3,000 and 4,000 years ago, a new people made their way south into the subcontinent from elsewhere. Their origins are not clear, but they are supposed to have come out of central Asia. Those newcomers were united by a language, which has come down to us as Sanskrit. They called themselves Aryans, a word hinting at nobility, high birth. The indigenous culture they met in the north of India was already

186

sophisticated. Archaeologists have called that older, local way of life Harappan, after one of its great cities, Harappa, which sprouted beside a tributary of the Indus River. Harappa was home to tens of thousands of people by 2250 BC. Modern excavation of buried ruins has revealed streets laid out on a carefully planned rectangular grid. Sophisticated irrigation watered their fields and drainage systems allowed for bathrooms in their houses. Each city had a citadel, a defended high point where people might gather in times of need.

Those Aryans were nomadic pastoralists and perhaps less polished in their ways than those among whom they had arrived. What they did have were horses and chariots, weapons of bronze and also a determination to stay. Archaeologists and anthropologists once speculated about an invasion, conquest. More recently the coming together of those different peoples has been described as migration, peaceful mixing. There were consequences just the same. The Harappans had been writers, keepers of records, but after the Aryans arrived that skill was lost for a thousand years and more, perhaps on account of a coarsening of society, a reversal that precluded such specialization and sophistication. City-living foundered too and had to be relearned much later, and in a rougher, less organized form than before. Climate change may have played a part – so that once fertile land was laid waste, forcing the abandonment of cities in river valleys for tougher lives elsewhere. The incomers were sacrificers of animals, worshippers of fire. Over time, their way of making sense of the cosmos mixed and fused with whatever had been the thinking of the Harappans. The result was finally greater than the sum of the parts, and laid the foundations for the way of life described as Hindu.

Fire was at the heart of life for those Aryans, presided over by a priestly class called Brahmans, who kept themselves apart. They sang hymns about gods, especially Varuna, who they believed controlled the heavens above and made order out of chaos, and a warrior called Indra who, in the hottest part of each year, went to war with and slaughtered a giant dragon to release the blessed rains of the monsoon. The hymns and other recitations of the Aryans were ancient by the time they arrived in India, learned by heart by their descendants and passed on. Some time around the end of the second millennium BC, these songs were written down in a vast collection called the *Rig-Veda*. The Brahmans guarded the sacred recitations and shared them only with their own. No others were to know the words. In this separation lay the foundations of the caste system, by which every man, woman and child was classified and taught their place. In the beginning there were divisions only between priests, warriors and peasant farmers – and it was possible to move between them. In time, after many centuries, the caste system became rigid, so that there were (and still are today) thousands of castes and a person had no earthly hope of moving from one to another.

In Sanskrit the god of fire is Agni (the root that gives the spark to 'ignite' in English), and in Kerala, a sect of those Brahmans called Nambudiri was minded (metaphorically speaking) to keep blowing on the coals of Agni for thousands of years. In any event, the rituals persisted. Part of the speaking of Sanskrit were forms called mantras – streams of sounds, elegantly structured like mathematical equations, and repeating like choruses in music. They were an intrinsic part of rituals, and in Kerala the ritual most deeply embedded, most carefully remembered, was Athirathram – the fire ritual for Agni.

Athirathram, known as the Kerala Fire Ritual, takes twelve days to perform in full. It was last completed in its entirety in 1975, in the village of Panjal, near Shoranur, at the request of Indologist Frits Staal, professor of philosophy at the University of California. In 2011 an abbreviated performance was paid for by wealthy Indian businessmen, but the truth is that this ritual, passed down the generations for hundreds of centuries by word of mouth alone, is teetering on the abyss of forgetting. In fundamental ways it may be lost already.

It is estimated that a whole language is lost every couple of weeks, with the death of some last elder speaker. Along with the vocabulary and the grammar goes a unique and irreplaceable way of comprehending the universe and what it means to be here on Earth. Athirathram is fading too, like fabric once bright but left too long in the sun.

The fire ritual is all about making and doing for the sake of making and doing. Sacred places, enclosures of poles roofed with rattan, are built to house the proceedings. According to tradition, the god Prajapati made the world and was unmade by the effort, reduced to fragments. Much of the activity of the ritual centres around the building of a large, flat altar of specially made clay bricks – squares, rectangles and triangles – assembled piece by piece to form the shape of a great bird of prey, a falcon, facing east, Prajapati made anew and ready to take flight towards the rising sun. All the while the ritual plays out; day and night, the Brahman priests recite the mantras.

A documentary called *Altar of Fire*, made by Professor Staal, exists online. It records that last performance by those Nambudiri of Kerala in 1975. Accompanying the images of the ritual are the priestly voices, droning and keening. Featured too are shots of a young boy learning the mantras by rote, carrying on the tradition. Father and son sit cross-legged, facing each other. With his hand the elder moves the younger's head rhythmically backward and forward, from side to side, the movement seeming to aid the process of remembering by the development of muscle memory. The boy's fingers flick reflexively in some count of verses. At the end of the ritual, the enclosures are set alight, consumed by fire. Onlookers jostle for glimpses of the destruction.

The effect is mesmerizing and otherworldly, alien even. Hardest of all to comprehend are the mantras (a Sanskrit word meaning something like 'tools for thinking'). Anthropologists, palaeontologists and the like have suggested language itself came late in the day to the human story. When those emigrants set out from Africa, they may have been people without words. The Neanderthals may well have been speechless too, and all of our ancient cousins before them.

According to Professor Staal, before speech there was ritual; patterned behaviour, instinctive and compulsive. Maybe human rituals have roots in behaviour like the mating dances of birds or the swarming of insects. As well as before language, ritual may also have come before meaning; our ancestors might have created and repeated acts and patterns only for the sake of doing so or for simple enjoyment. Much later, according to Staal, after the advent of language, we sought to work backwards through time, seeking meaning where there was none. Some traditions, actions and behaviours are older even than meaning.

When the fire ritual was recorded in 1975, the mantras in particular perplexed the witnesses from the western world. The English mathematician Alan Turing is said to have perceived the underlying matrix of the Athirathram, building his first computers upon its scaffold. Among the mantras are sequences, passages, patterns and cadences that have no translation into Sanskrit or any other language. When questioned, the priests could say only that the sounds were 'handed down'. A possible explanation came when the mantras were analysed by Staal to find parallels in nature. Their closest equivalent was found to be birdsong. It has been suggested that some of the sounds within the mantras of the Kerala Fire Ritual are those our species made in the time before words, before language. As language developed it may have inadvertently collected, scooped up older sounds, like seeds picked up in a ball of dough as it is worked on a board. The Athirathram may be so old, its recitations passed down through the years by faithful repetition alone, that it holds fossilized within it the sounds we made when we communicated one to another like the birds of the air, the beasts of the forest.

Some people spend lifetimes in existential agony, trying to make sense of the world and the universe. Whatever moved our ancestors to walk away from the places where they were born – in a time before speech – they may have been untroubled by the meaning of it all. Like migratory birds or wandering herds they moved in response to external

190

and internal stimuli, in time with earthly and universal rhythms we no longer feel. Even now our every action, for good or ill, is part of the making and remaking of the universe – nothing more and nothing less. Every gesture is a contribution, for good or ill. For some thousands of years we have remembered stories and told them to each other. Since we have no way of knowing when our species woke up, gained consciousness for the first time, we cannot say how old the oldest stories are. Before stories, before meaning, there was only action. Our earliest ancestors walked and created, lived and died in a time before consciousness itself. We do not have to understand it all. For the longest time it was actions, even unconscious actions, that made all the difference. Quite recently in the scheme of things we made stories to make sense of the actions, the movements, the comings and goings. Action for good is more important than any story we might tell. Stories are words and words are vital; it is how we live every moment that matters even more. It is miracle enough to be here. What we have is the time and the chance to do something, make something, to live a life. In that time allotted to us we could at least make and live something good.

Lindisfarne Gospels
– death and birth

They arise, serene and unetiolated, one by one
from their subterranean sleep of five long years.

— HOPE MIRRLEES,
'Paris: A Poem'

I F ONLY ONE thing in this book lodges in the memory, consider
this: the Lindisfarne Gospels weighs the same as an adult badger.

Crafted of vellum – sheets of parchment made from the skins of
more than a hundred calves – and weighing nearly 19lb, it is a holy
book made on the island of Lindisfarne, in Northumberland. The Gospels in question are New Testament – those according to Matthew,
Mark, Luke and John. They are stories remembered and endlessly retold
for 2,000 years. Unlike most medieval manuscripts, the Lindisfarne
Gospels features an explanation for its own existence: it was the work
of Bishop Eadfrith early in the eighth century.

Art experts revere the book as a masterpiece. It is home-grown too,
born of the form of Christianity that had taken root and sprung up in
the west of Britain and Ireland in the middle centuries of the first millennium after Christ. It is also made of the immutable, undeniable
constituent elements and atoms of the north of England – and not just

the calfskins. They used to say the necessary pigments had come from far off – lapis lazuli from the Mediterranean, yellow orpiment from Afghanistan – but now there are specialists who insist the colours are from local sources.

Rome had embraced Christianity, happily or not, by the fourth century, but the fall of the empire in the fifth century saw the old pagan ways sprout like weeds. In the early years, Christianity had been a religion of the towns anyway, carried along the roads (our oldest built structures) by holy men. Off the beaten tracks, out of sight and mind, the old gods had lingered furtively. With no soldiers on the roads, and less traffic of any sort, the pagans crept back into the light. Christianity was pushed to the fringes and clung there like ivy to forgotten nooks and crannies. After an exile of a century or so it quietly returned to mainland Britannia. By AD 563 the Irish priest Columba was on the Hebridean island of Iona, seeking to re-seed the word of his God. A bishop from Iona – Aidan – came to Lindisfarne in 635 at the invitation of Oswald, king of Northumbria. It was thus a Hibernian, Celtic version of Christianity – not Roman – and its style was reflected in great works of devotion such as the Lindisfarne Gospels.

Bishop Eadfrith was inspired by his own vision and created something with the power to enrapture readers and non-readers alike. For those who could not be moved by the Latin words alone, there were illuminated pages touched by grace. The depictions of the Evangelists are startling now as they surely were then – an angel for Matthew, a lion for Mark, a bull-calf for Luke and an eagle for John. Throughout are illustrations and geometrical designs of hypnotizing power, beguiling and enthralling. One page of Luke's Gospel has upon it more than 10,000 dots of red ink – their creation an entire day's work.

The Lindisfarne Gospels is not the only work of its kind. The Book of Kells, the Durham Gospels, the Book of Durrow – all of them and more bear witness to faith as inspiration. Books and stories mattered to those men, and unlike churches and cathedrals they could be moved when need arose. In 875, with Vikings prowling, the monks of Lindisfarne upped and left their island refuge. Taking the Gospels with them, and the bones of their greatest saint, Cuthbert, they set out on a journey that lasted 200 years. All over the north of England they roamed, those monks and their successors, stopping in countless places that still bear Cuthbert's name or his nickname, Cuddy. By the time a cathedral was built for him at Durham, the Gospels and the bones had wound a thousand miles.

'In the beginning was the word . . .' it says in John, the conclusion being that spoken truth conjures order out of the chaos of nothingness. Chaos was what had threatened and been held at bay during the years of religious decline, but only just. Christianity was 700 years old by the time Eadfrith made an eagle of John, symbolic of the resurrected God, and by then another faith was awake in the world. Far away in the east, in 610, Muhammad had begun reciting the stories he said the Archangel Gabriel had taught him in a cave near Mecca. By the time the bishop was making his dots of red on vellum in the scriptorium on Lindisfarne, the followers of Islam had long since committed other stories to memory.

Christianity feels old now, and for 1,400 years it has shared this Earth with Islam. The younger faith was dynamic from the off, driven. Muhammad submitted to God (Islam means 'submission') and recited what he had heard. The message was potent, and within fifty years the old classical world was all but submerged by the rising waters of the new religion. Western Christianity had retreated all the while – to Lindisfarne and Iona, to Skellig Michael and Ireland. It was books and stories that kept Christianity alive during the uncertainty of years when it might have vanished.

They are hard to visualize, those priests who came out of the old world in the first centuries of Christianity. Shadowy as any band of ice-age hunters, they may have followed some of the same ancient roads across the world. They came out of the Holy Land and followed the setting sun into the west. Some of them took their inspiration from Anthony the Great and the Desert Fathers of the third and fourth centuries. Eschewing all but the company of God, those founders of the monastic tradition had chosen lonely lives in the Egyptian desert. Their ascetic ways were practised next in the eastern Mediterranean and then carried into France – to Marseilles and Tours and onwards to old Britannia. Those descriptions of the wanderers that do exist have them wearing their hair long at the back but shaved to stubble forwards of the crown. They wore plain robes and sought the edges of the world. What impression they made on arrival in the British Isles may only be guessed at. Yet they survived, gained footholds. They built communities for themselves, monasteries, buildings of wood and turf, and lived the hardest lives imaginable. Some of them were craftsmen, able to work in precious metals and polished stones that caught the eyes of the kings and warlords they encountered, and whose patronage and protection they required. At least as important, perhaps more so, they could write, putting on to parchment and into stone the words of those kings and chiefs. Once settled and at peace in places like Iona and Lindisfarne they copied their remembered stories into new books and made covers for them of gold and glittering stones.

The religion they followed, the word they obeyed, was only seven centuries old – no time at all, and it was all but swept away in those years remembered as the Dark Ages. Its resilient foundations were forged of stories and memory, and they stayed in place. The whole of western civilization is raised on those foundations. Our laws and moral code are fused with the lowest layers, cut into the bedrock billions of years old. As long as 1,400 years ago the structure needed rebuilding almost from the ground up.

We are renovating our house in Stirling. Like a majority of the inhabitants of modern Britain we live in Victorian housing stock that has lasted longer than was ever intended. We maintain our small part of it, replacing the electrics and the plumbing, replastering walls and ceilings and painting them in new colours. We uncover fireplaces and line chimneys. We check the roof and refurbish the windows to make the whole wind- and water-tight – but it is the same old house, on old foundations out of sight. All our work is an act of memory, active remembering of what has been there, what is worthy of remaining. Rather than just a story, the house is something solid and real, made of positive action.

Without our attention or someone else's, the house would fall into disrepair, and then fall down altogether. Civilizations fall down. The Egyptian, the Greek, the Roman – all faltered and failed. Our civilization is as vulnerable. Either it will be revivified somehow, ashen, etiolated skin flushed pink by new blood, or not.

It may all feel naive now, the way of those early Christians. How could they have believed what they did? Why did they live and die for stories? But believe they did, and what remained after they were gone was the hard shell after the soft living thing within has died. The loved body dies and is laid in the ground and hundreds of years later the lifeless bones are still as hard as scaffolding poles.

The civilization we take for granted does not float in mid-air as a mote of dust. Rather we are held aloft by a calcified skeleton made of history. Dry bones. Take that away and what will hold us up? Our world will not remain suspended without it.

From time to time there are attempts at tearing down the old towers of civilization, so they might be replaced with the prefabs and high-rise flats of revolution. Fascism, communism, socialism, even humanism – those and others have imagined new worlds. The experiments have not worked so far and have never replaced the old values with anything better. As it turns out we are not good at inventing new values, even after all this time.

Western civilization has been badly wounded, in the last hundred years or so especially. During the twentieth century it came close to bleeding to death. When the guns fell silent in 1918 there was genuine concern that France – or the entity that had been the French nation – might have been hurt too badly to survive. Two million men lost. The shape on the map was still there, but it had been bled dry. Somehow, some version of France was made to stand up and march again. That century advanced, new values were adopted in places such as the Soviet Union, China, Cambodia and others besides, and tens of millions died.

It may be that a civilization that has sustained and been around for thousands of years has been around too long, outstayed its welcome. It is all made of stories, versions of stories that are older than imperial Rome, older than classical Greece, and that have been told and retold. Characters' names may have changed but the essential truth of the stories has remained the same. Maybe the ideas have been worn too thin now – made transparent, too ragged to provide warmth.

And yet our way of life has survived the very worst. After the carnage of that First World War, survivors sought high places where they could breathe clean air, untainted by the stench of mutilated death. In *Into the Silence*, Canadian anthropologist Wade Davis described the Herculean efforts of British climbers to summit Everest in the years just after that war. In the vanguard were men who had seen and survived what had hitherto been unimaginable. Their spirits had been tested and sometimes broken. Men raised in the Church never set foot in such places after the war, never stood again for the National Anthem. Men like George Mallory had watched the innocent Edwardian world of younger years blown to smithereens, soaked in blood. Dying on the rock of Everest held no comparable fear for him and his ilk because they had spent years watching other men of their generation daily crossing the 'frail barrier' of death, 'smiling and gallant'.

Friedrich Nietzsche had predicted the death of God in the nineteenth century. Between 1914 and 1918, men and women believed they had watched it happen, seen the corpse fall cold. In 1922 T. S. Eliot published *The Waste Land*. His misery and hopelessness about the state of civilization, of life itself, are palpable. Among much else, he mourned

197

the rise of technology of the sort that had industrialized the slaughter of the war at the seeming expense of matters cultural and spiritual. Hope Mirrlees was another Modernist poet but in 'Paris', a poem written in 1919, she saw the glimmer of new life beyond the apocalypse. She described the shattering of the city, the attendant death, but also the signs of resurrection:

> The sun is rising,
> Soon Les Halles will be open,
> The sky is saffron behind the two towers of Notre-Dame.

One hundred years later, Notre-Dame burned. But the walls and foundations remained and the cathedral will rise again. More than the embodiment of the religion that built it, Notre-Dame is a story, and it is stories that last longest. If our civilization is to continue, then it will be by remembering the stories we used to tell each other about the inevitability of death and the promise of rebirth.

10.

Echoes

Edwin's Sparrow
and appreciating small things

Happy the man whose wish and care
A few paternal acres bound,
Content to breathe his native air
In his own ground.

— ALEXANDER POPE,
'Ode on Solitude'

IN MY GARDEN there is a shrub gone out of control. Tough pale stalks, thin as fingers and twice my height, thumb-sized lime-green leaves edged with tiny teeth. Up close it has a dusty, musty scent like sun-warmed soil. To my shame I have no idea what sort it is. Late in the year it flowers white, celebrating its existence. It is a home for sparrows; they fill it with their chit-chat, darting in and out of their leafy tower block so that it fairly vibrates with the life of them. Of all birds, I like sparrows best. Small and drab; dun and black and chubby. They have been gifted little enough but they are doughty. They work hard to fly, those puddle jumpers of the avian world. Bursts of rise and fall, like a bouncing ball or a stone skimming water. You can almost feel the effort, even in their shortest flights. Stubby wings furious and thrumming. Sparrows have pluck. They get on with it.

Lately I have been looking round my home patch, noticing how much I have taken for granted, overlooked. The streets are tree-lined. I have walked in their shade in summer and by their wintry skeletons without bothering to know what species they are. It is the same with the flowers, wild on the verges and tame in the gardens, the same with most of the birds. On the horizon, glimpsed blue in gaps between the houses, are ancient mountains. I am not sure of their names either. One is Ben Lomond. Recently I have been reading about geology and botany, nipping off leaves and blossoms, pocketing them and taking them home to hold against illustrations, trying to learn and commit it all to memory. I am anxious about how much simple stuff I have not bothered to know.

The common knowledge we draw upon and take for granted feels as immemorial as mountains. It is easy to forget that other generations accepted an altogether different landscape, a landscape of the mind – viewing all about them through an older prism. Much of what we know or have been told came late in the day, relative to our own species. Only fourteen centuries ago, a blink, some of our ancestors encountered Christianity for the first time. It was a young thing and new – a blown seed and vulnerable, rootless at first and likely to be whipped away.

Spread up and down the east of England and Scotland (before there was an England or a Scotland) were once two kingdoms. They were Bernicia and Deira, made by Britons and Angles, locals and foreigners. In the seventh century AD they melded into one realm, Northumbria. To the south was Mercia, ruled by Penda. There were others – seven realms, making what historians called the Heptarchy. Those names of places and people feel foreign, suited to Tolkien or *Game of Thrones* – to elves and orcs and dragons. Foreign or not, strange or not, those were places and kings our ancestors knew as pagans.

Everyone worships something, and the earliest migrants from Germanic lands, across the grim grey water, raised altars to Odin, Thor, Loki and the rest. Vulnerable or not, the windblown seed of the

Christian religion caught among them, put down a shining tracery of roots here and there, and soon the kings were curious.

Theirs were kingdoms of farmers, planters and growers, subjects governed by years shaped by furrows in black soil, other seeds and seasons. Fields made by parents and grandparents, defined by banks of earth or low walls.

For thousands of years after the retreat of ice, Britain had been a forest – of aspen, birch and willow first, then oak, then ash, beech, elm, holly, hornbeam, lime, maple and more. I have always known the names yet struggle to identify one from another. When the Neolithic farmers first set to with axes of polished stone, it was still a wildwood of shadows, browsing deer dappled by light shattered into fragments by shivering leaves. By the middle of the last millennium BC half of these islands had been cleared of trees. The felling never stopped, and all who came poked more holes through the ceiling of green. Those Angles and their Saxon familiars were the busiest of all, of the greenest fingers. Small lives rooted in shires, landscapes from which men and women had few reasons to stray from one year to the next. Their world was small, but they knew it like the family they saw every day, and had names for everything and everyone.

From Bede's *Ecclesiastical History of the English People* we know Edwin was a king of Bernicia and Deira from AD 616. Some time around 627, King Edwin was minded to find a different god to worship. A holy man named Paulinus came to him and suggested he might follow the Christian way. Edwin was cautious and gathered his best men and invited them to discuss the offer with him.

One of them thought a while and said: 'Your Majesty, when we compare the present life of man on Earth with that time of which we have no knowledge, it seems to me like the swift flight of a single sparrow through the banqueting-hall where you are sitting at dinner on a winter's day with your counsellors. In the midst there is a comforting fire to warm the hall; outside, the storms of winter rain or snow are raging. The sparrow flies swiftly in through one door of the hall and out through another. While he is inside, he is safe from the winter storms; but after a few moments of comfort, he vanishes from sight into the wintry world from which he came. Even so, man appears on Earth for a little while; but of what went before this life or what follows, we know nothing. Therefore, if this new teaching has brought any more certain knowledge, it seems only right that we should follow it.'

It was a powerful image the adviser conjured, of a hall, a fire and a sparrow's flight. That thane of Edwin's understood that life is brief. As well as brief it is shadowed, ahead and behind, by the darkness of the unknowable. Even that bright span of moments, made warm by life, is more than most of us have time to notice in full, its everyday details. Matthew's Gospel has it that though the price of a pair of sparrows is a single copper coin, not one falls without God knowing it and why. Regardless of faith, or the lack of it, the message is that each of us has value in the universe, and the same value, just as every sparrow is seen and counted.

Edwin opted for the new religion, an alternative map for a landscape of the mind, a new way to see it and navigate it. The *Anglo-Saxon Chronicle* records his baptism at Easter 627, at York – he and all his people with him. He ordered the building of a church, first in timber and then stone. This is often the way – a soldier's grave remembered with a wooden cross, replaced later with Portland stone. First living wood then everlasting rock of the Earth, first windblown seed then mountain. Edwin saw Paulinus called archbishop. In October 633, after he had been king seventeen years, he was defeated and killed in battle at Haethfield (Hatfield, by Doncaster) by Penda of Mercia.

As well as books about geology, animals and birds I read others about history. All I ever seem to learn is that I do not, cannot, know enough. I am reassured by sparrows, reminded by their brief flight that time is short and effort is required to make the most of whatever is available. Nothing is too small, too brief for meaning. John Muir, explorer and naturalist – Scots-born founder of America's National Parks – wrote over a century ago, in *My First Summer in the Sierra*, 'when we try to pick out anything by itself, we find it hitched to everything else in the universe'.

I am paying attention to trees and sparrows. I can know the names of the things I see every day, and so see them properly and accord them their due. We are on Earth a little while, but of what went before this life or what follows, we know nothing. Life is brief and every one thing is hitched to everything else. Wordsworth said the meanest flower that blows gave him thoughts that lie 'too deep for tears'. It might be enough to know and appreciate the contents of one garden.

The Flow Country
– shadows on the moor and lost languages

Your noble body's blood,
Lying on the ground.
Your sweet body's blood,
Through the linen was soaking.
Sucking it was I,
'Til I choked for breath.

– A MHIC IAIN 'IC SHEUMAIS
(traditional Gaelic poem)

IN THE SUMMER of 2019 I spent some days in Scotland's far north-east, in the wilderness called the Flow Country. Some pronounce 'Flow' to rhyme with 'go'; others with 'plough', which is a reminder of the Norse *floi*, meaning 'marshy'. The lack of consensus is fitting, part of a pattern of vagueness and forgetting. Tracing the outline of the Flow Country, which straddles the counties of Caithness and Sutherland, is like pinpointing Brigadoon: folk know it is there but seldom agree on its precise position on the map. It all heightens the misty, mysterious nature of the place.

The Flow Country covers around 1,500 square miles; twice the area of Orkney, it is the largest expanse of blanket bog in the whole of Europe. Blanket bog is not the most romantic of names, redolent as it is of splashy, sucking glaur and pungent smells. The connotations of the handle are unfortunate, for such terrain has qualities bordering on the mythical.

Blanket bog forms where rainfall is so heavy that the water builds up faster than it can be evaporated by wind and sunlight. Some plants favour the perpetual sogginess and so thrive among the puddles. When they die, the remains do not rot (on account of the prevailing acidic, anaerobic conditions) but accumulate instead. Layer by layer the vegetation grows thicker, forming peat. It is like a blanket, filling not just dips and hollows but spreading for mile after square mile, up hill and down dale. Any organic material within the peat – fallen trees, seeds, pollen grains, dead creatures great and small – all of it is liable to languish, smothered and preserved beyond the reach of corruption. Instead of recycling there is hoarding. Trapped beyond the grasp of time, sound and deep is the sleep beneath that blanket.

The Flow Country has been growing in Caithness and Sutherland since the end of the last ice age and is, in places, more than 30 feet deep. For much of the time it makes for mournful, featureless terrain and muted colours – dun, grey and brown, dotted with pools that either reflect the sky in whichever mood or else, on account of the tannin in the water, shine black and impenetrable as crude oil. It can be a hard place to love, hard even to notice. For the most part, travellers in cars flit around its edges, unaware the Flow Country even exists as a place. It can seem more absence than presence.

And then . . . then there are moments, minutes, fleeting as happiness, when the elements conspire to conjure a shimmering, shape-shifting performance artwork of ethereal loveliness across the water. Much of it is about light – changing patterns of shade and contrast. In their season there are all manner of flowers too, offering scattered pinpricks of colour: pink bell heather; white common cotton grass; yellow bog asphodel; purple butterwort; sphagnum mosses of many tones; perfect white stars of chickweed; tiny antlers of grey-green lichen.

Bright as any flower (and as vulnerable to extinction, as it turns out) is the Gaelic language of Scotland – another living thing grown from the landscape and nursed by weather. Sprung from mountain, moor and flood, it expresses the forms and mercurial moods of the places of its cradling more sensitively by far than the English language that has supplanted it. Among a countless treasure trove are *rionnach maiom*, which describes the shadow-patterns of fast-moving clouds cast upon a moor by sunlight on a windy day; *tioradh*, the interval between curtains of rain sweeping in from the sea; and *na luin*, a shimmering heat haze flitting quickly over the moor. Gaelic is a gentle litany of words and sounds – the secret selves of places, things and atmospheres made manifest. But landscapes and languages must not be taken for granted. Each is as vulnerable as the other to forgetting and loss.

I made my own visit to the Flow Country in support of a long, ongoing campaign to have the whole area named a World Heritage site. The push has been underway for years and has more to go before any decision is likely from UNESCO. Surprising numbers of people crowded into town halls and school assembly halls in Thurso, Wick and Inverness to hear speakers like me preach the importance of a wonder hiding in plain sight. Some spoke of the living place and the living things that thrive there. I was there as an archaeologist, to talk about all the lingering fingerprints of mankind. Since the place is not my own I felt incongruous, an interloper. But by its very nature the land of the blanket bog is muffled and in need of voices to speak up for it. The Flow Country is a cache of evidence about the lives of our ancestors. Standing stones, chambered tombs of the dead and houses for the living are folded into the matrix, slowly being swallowed. Everywhere I went I heard tales of people lost for ever in the peatlands, believed to have been enveloped by this pool or that and never seen again. Before the peat, the terrain was populated by farmers of crops and animals and it is those lives that hide there. A thousand stories of lives lived are lying waiting, safe. The peat is a far more effective carbon store than any rainforest. By preserving such environments we keep the planet cooler than it might otherwise be. Blanket bog matters to the future as well as to the past.

The Flow Country was properly under threat in the 1970s and 1980s when, in a bid to create employment and exploit the potential of the emptiness, countless conifers were planted by the Forestry Commission. Tax breaks encouraged the wealthy to invest in it all until campaigners persuaded the then Conservative government to pull the plug. The inducement was removed and the planting stopped, but damage already done by the digging of miles upon miles of drains is still evident. That place is not mine and yet its fate should be of interest to all of us, since to forget an entire landscape would be yet another symptom of the distance forming between ourselves and the natural world outside.

I speak no Gaelic either, but I need to know that that ancient language will survive in the landscape that summoned it into being. Gaelic – an older language of the north, though not the oldest – is withering even in its heartland of the Western Isles, drying out, drained by the enervating cuckoo of English. Professor Rob Dunbar, chair of Celtic languages at the University of Edinburgh, has spoken of his concern. 'The number of children from Gaelic-speaking homes seems to be declining and we are now at a point where just a bare majority of the population are Gaelic-speaking,' he told *The Herald* newspaper in 2017. 'Based on the numbers of young people learning the language, it won't be long until Gaelic speakers are a minority in the Western Isles. It raises questions about whether parents are passing on the language and, in these circumstances, the long-term viability of the language on the islands is in serious trouble.'

Gaelic was spoken all over Scotland once upon a time, having itself replaced some older Celtic tongue. The winnowing in the Western Isles now is only the latest instalment of a story that has been unfolding for hundreds of years.

Just as the Flow Country holds the stuff of the past, so the Gaelic language is an irreplaceable memory of landscape. Its speakers were wedded to the land, subject to the elements. As we lose their words, so we discard the cargo of understanding they carried. They were farmers and hunters and needed to be able to communicate to one another every nuance of a fluid, changeful world. An expanse like the Flow Country appears featureless at first sight, miles and miles of bugger all. But for those whose lives were lived in part upon it, detailed, precise use of language made it possible to carry maps in the mind and to project them on to the land when needed. In a radio interview the Canadian anthropologist and author Wade Davis once spoke about how a language 'is not just a grammar or a vocabulary, a language is a flash of the human spirit . . . an old growth forest of the mind'. By conveying difference, detail and nuance, inhabitants might share among them an understanding and appreciation that infused the emptiness with form and meaning. 'The hardest thing of all to see,' the nature writer J. A. Baker remarked in his 1967 work *The Peregrine*, 'is what is really there.'

The lines quoted at the start of this chapter are from an old Gaelic poem about the wounding of one Donald MacIain 'Ic Sheumais – Donald, son of John, son of James – at the Battle of Carinish on North Uist, in 1601. Shot through by an arrow, he was tended afterwards by one of his womenfolk. In the old way of thinking, blood – life itself – comes from the land. In death, the blood must return. For those who love the land and live close to it, there is often a profound sense of communion. Rather than let that settlement of debt get underway too soon, Donald's woman supped his spilled blood and took it into herself, rather than see it return prematurely to the land. As we spend more and more time in the manmade, built environment, we break and lose track of this fundamental connection to the earth. It has survived in Scotland so far in the reservoir of the Gaelic language, but that tongue is being bled white.

Some historians track the decline all the way back to the marriage of King Malcolm III – Malcolm Canmore – to the Anglo-Saxon princess Margaret of Wessex in 1070. She spoke no Gaelic and furthermore encouraged her husband to invite English-speaking nobles and Churchmen into his kingdom. Margaret is remembered as a saint – the Pearl of Scotland – but she set at least one unhappy trend. By the end of the fifteenth century the rot set in and Gaelic fell from favour altogether. From time to time, kings of Scotland had been challenged, directly or indirectly, by the Lords of the Isles, rulers of an all-but-independent sea kingdom rooted in the islands in the west. In 1462 John MacDonald, Lord of the Isles, sided with the English king Edward IV in a bid for control of Scotland. It was a secret bond until 1493, when James IV, King of Scots, learned of the betrayal, seized the Lordship out from under John MacDonald and kept it for himself and his heirs ever after. Since the folk of the Lordship had spoken in Gaelic, plotted against the Scottish crown in Gaelic, the language itself was singled out, scapegoated as the tongue of traitors. Thus traduced, it has been in terminal decline, drip by drip, ever since.

It seems to me that lessons are to be learned not just from the acts of ancient people, but also from the ancient places that cradled them, the words they used in their bid for understanding. The landscape was there before the people. In time, the people came and their lives were shaped by the places. The places shaped their language too; demanded it from them if they were to make sense of their world and share it with one another. Wisdom is there in the words that were spoken then. In Scotland, it was Gaelic that made sense of that world before English. The Flow Country holds the past 10,000 years in its depths; Gaelic holds the older, better sense of the land. Before any more is lost we should do whatever is necessary to save and revivify those ancient languages that still survive in the world. Their loss is a rising of the floodwater, every word forgotten the snuffing out of a spark of inspiration. We need all the language we can get.

Tiwi Islands
and the invention of death

They question each other, the young, the golden hearted,
Of the world that they were robbed of in
their quiet paradise.

— HUMBERT WOLFE,
'Requiem: The Soldier'

A COUPLE OF YEARS ago I missed a flight from Snake Bay Airport in the Tiwi Islands, in Australia's Northern Territory. My intended destination was Darwin, only 50 or so miles away across a ribbon of ocean, but 50 miles can be a long way in the wild places of the world. It was late in the day when I was dropped off, the sun low in the sky. There are no staff at Snake Bay Airport. Darkness fell so fast I almost heard it hit the ground. Only then did I bother to think about checking details. I looked at my phone, my only light source, and saw a battery level of 4 per cent. Anxiety flicked in my gut like a lizard's tail.

Snake Bay Airport is on Melville Island. The other Tiwi Island of any size is Bathurst, and both are mere dots of territory marooned from mainland Australia around 8,000 years ago, as sea levels rose after the last ice age. They are home to the Tiwi people, an indigenous group of around 2,500, separate and distinct from their continental neighbours. There is not much to Snake Bay Airport. In truth it is a brick-built, covered gateway through a tall chain-link fence on to an airstrip carved out of the bush. On the walls are brightly coloured paintings – Aboriginal art, of turtles and sharks, an indication of what the Tiwi Islanders used to hunt and eat long ago.

My trip to the airfield had taken around forty minutes through thick bush, along a dirt track that had been a challenge even for a 4×4. The thought of heading back along that track on foot in moonless darkness, past waterways known to be home to saltwater crocodiles, was unappealing. I entered the number for the production coordinator back in Sydney, thousands of miles (and a whole world) away, and pressed the green button. Mercifully she answered on the third ring. I explained my circumstances.

'Leave it with me,' she said.

She hung up before I could tell her about my phone battery. I looked at the screen and saw 2 per cent.

Suffice it to say my phone, my only timepiece, died while I waited. I felt like I had been lying in the dark for half the night wondering what sound, if any, an approaching saltie might make when the runway landing lights clicked on by themselves. It was like something from *Close Encounters of the Third Kind*, a blindingly bright triangle of light stretching off into the invisible. I heard the sound of an approaching aircraft – one that had, as it turned out, been re-routed on my behalf by an apologetic charter airline brought up to speed, by my production coordinator, about my abandonment on the edge of the universe.

Among a mix of emotions, the runway lights and the aircraft noise inspired in me that night a feeling of having returned to the known world from a place or a time far away. I was just 50 miles from the bright lights, the big city of Darwin, but alone in the dark in the Australian bush in the middle of a tropical island I could have been in any time in the history of the world. From that perspective I was effectively outside time. Lying on a wooden bench and looking into infinity, my mind had made space for dreams. In the absence of a mobile phone, and the rest of the modern world, dreams had been as real as anything else.

On the Tiwi Islands the story everyone knows is about Purrukapali, his wife Bima and their baby son Jinani. Every day, Bima went into the forest to gather food, carrying Jinani with her. She was having a passionate affair with Purrukapali's brother, Japara, and there came a fateful day when he persuaded her to leave Jinani lying in the shade of a tree while they made love nearby. Time passed, the sun moved in the sky, and what had been shade became too bright, too hot, and the baby died of exposure. Purrukapali found his son's body and saw at once what had happened. He attacked Bima first, beating her about the head with his throwing stick. She fled deeper into the forest while he turned his wrath on Japara. The men fought savagely, finally reaching a beach by the sea where Japara tried to appease his brother by promising he could bring the baby back to life after three days. Purrukapali did not believe him. Walking backwards into the water, his dead son in his arms, he cried out, 'You must follow me. As I die, so must everyone and everything.' Purrukapali and Jinani disappeared beneath the waves. Before that moment, death had not existed in the world; thereafter it was inevitable for all of creation. Shamed by what he had caused, Japara turned himself into the moon. Even though he is reincarnated every month, he must die for three days in each. Bima turned herself into a curlew and the cries of the bird at night are those of a mother mourning her dead son for eternity.

In recent years, a new darkness has descended on the Tiwi Islands. Just as it has for indigenous people all over Australia, two and a half centuries of contact with European settlers has taken a dreadful toll. The incomers – first Dutch, then Portuguese, then British – were kept at bay at first, at least on the Tiwi Islands. Spear-throwing warriors discouraged all contact until the second decade of the twentieth century, when a Christian mission landed, took root and set about undermining millennia of isolation and tradition. By the time a Labor government sought to restore some of the islanders' traditional rights in the 1970s, the old ways were irreparably damaged. The mission was disempowered but drink and drugs were sucked into the vacuum created by its absence. Along with addiction has come one of the highest rates of suicide in the world. By some estimates one in four islanders has attempted to take his or her life. Funerals are frequent in the place where death was allegedly invented.

Tiwis have, since time immemorial, made and planted poles to mark the graves of their dead. These are carved of ironwood, painted with black charcoal, white clay and red or yellow ochre, and called *tutini*. Like route markers, they help the spirits find their way to the next world. On the Tiwi Islands too many spirits are lost, those of the living as well as of the dead. The lessons of the past that gave meaning to life have been unlearned. The elders, who remembered the time before, who knew and could explain, are gone.

The days of hunting and gathering are past. There is precious little work, for precious little money. Some effort has been made to encourage the making of art and crafts for sale to the tourists who pass through. Much of life revolves around so-called social clubs where alcohol is for sale. Every adult knows exactly how many cans he or she is permitted, by law, to buy. It is hard to say what positive effect, if any, the rationing has. Outside the clubs, beyond the wire perimeters, prowl the many who have been barred for some transgression or other. When the beer has all been drunk everyone goes home. And yet, for many, home is a place of fear, of violence and rape fuelled by intoxication of one form or another.

When everyone is utterly befuddled, it is then that Purrukapali comes back to haunt them. They still remember him, for all the good he does them now. What had been a story about man, woman and the responsibilities of both has become an inducement, an encouragement to die. A timeless legend that explained the birth of the moon, the cry of the curlew and the inescapable knowledge that death must follow life has been corrupted into hopelessness. It was a story about beginnings, now it inspires only the end. What the Tiwis had is all but gone, reduced to faint echoes. Only a few can talk about the ghosts called *mapurtiti* that are held at arm's length by the *tutini* poles, about the little spirit people called *nyingawi*, about the *yamparriparri* who fly in the sky looking for lost Tiwis to eat. The fragments seem slight and foolish, tales to beguile children.

In the time that passed while I waited in the dark at Snake Bay Airport I thought about the invention of death. So much of our understanding of the universe and our place within it has been provided for us by those who went before – long, long before. We know about past and future, of course we do. We have also had it explained to us that we are born to an unknown, unknowable span of life, and that death must follow. Somehow the days, months and years in between must be filled. It is important to remember that all of those ideas had to be shaped at some time, those profound concepts framed and put into words that the many might understand. The shape and texture of reality is not obvious, far from it. Architects of artificial intelligence have had to concede that reality and existence are so unfathomably complicated they can scarcely begin to understand how we humans are able to perceive it, let alone make some sense of it.

It is also instructive to bear witness to what happens when ideas die and when our species outlives the explanations that worked once upon a time. Stories do not have to be true, far less scientific, in order to matter. The Tiwis functioned as a society of some sort for an unimaginably long time; they maintained and sustained themselves until just before the outbreak of the First World War. For all our cleverness, we have undone all of that. It may be that the Tiwis are canaries in the coalmine. Once they knew a whole universe, real and imagined, that worked for them and explained it all. Part of their belief was in ghosts, little people and flying monsters. Silly or not (to our eyes, at least), they gave life meaning and kept people whole and sane and sober for tens of thousands of years. Now they have beer, dope and suicide. We have done away with most of what our ancestors believed, holy ghosts and all, and now we in our turn rattle with painkillers, anti-depressants, beta-blockers, statins and sleeping pills. Like the Tiwis, we evidently need more than scientific facts. We need something to believe. The ideologies of the twentieth century cut down the old forests of the mind where all the answers lived. Like the orangutan and the jaguar, hope is an endangered species. We need our own *tutini* poles to keep the dead and death at bay.

11.

Loss

Vedbaek

– a mother and a baby and living life in hope

First to our ancestors who lie in barrows
Or under nameless cairns on heathery hills
Or where the seal-swim crashes the island narrows . . .
To all, clay-bound or chalk-bound, stiff or scattered,
We leave the values of their periods,
The things that seemed to them the things that mattered.

— W. H. AUDEN AND LOUIS MACNEICE,
'Their Last Will and Testament',
in *Letters from Iceland*

Y EARS AGO, when I was a student, one of my lecturers recounted a story about archaeologists finding an amphora, 2,500 years old, filled to the brim with honey, and tasting it and finding it still good. Out of sight at first but visible within after a while was the body of a baby, enshrouded by the sweetness, untouched by time and perfectly preserved by the magic of bees and by ageless love. This is how our species thinks; in this and countless other ways we try to make sense of reality, make it tolerable for our human minds. Thinking like a

221

scientist – a skill so recently acquired by *Homo sapiens* – is so hard, so demanding, it has to be learned and practised assiduously. Even scientists are able to think like scientists only for short periods. For the rest of us, the true texture of reality is out of reach. We take more comfort from love and honey.

Mesolithic is the word used by archaeologists to describe the ways of the last of the hunters. Etymologically speaking it means the middle Stone Age. It is a filling of uncertain flavour in an asymmetric sandwich – between the thick slice that is the Palaeolithic old Stone Age and the thin slice of upwardly mobile new Stone Age called the Neolithic. For several thousand years, as the glaciers and ice sheets of the last ice age waxed and waned, then diminished and finally vanished, our hunter ancestors persevered. The technology of farming would come soon enough, learned first by others of their kind in the Middle East some 10,000 years ago. For the first six millennia or so after the ice retreated however, life for humankind was much as it had always been.

Like a great deal of the northern hemisphere, the landmass we know today as Scandinavia had spent a frigid aeon beneath a cap of ice almost a mile thick. By 12,000 years ago it seems there were signs of recovery; a thready pulse and the flickerings of a return to life. The north began to wake up. It was touch and go, progress made in fits and starts, temperatures rising and falling. After two more millennia there came a time of sustained and settled improvement, the mercury always on the rise as it were. The planet's hibernation (which is Latin for 'the occupation of winter quarters') was over.

Trees like aspen, birch and sallow, thrifty and adaptable, gained a toehold first and then spread, blurring and softening a landscape that had been composed of fractured rock and sullen, wind-lashed, frostbitten morass. Later arboreal arrivals – elm, hazel, oak – provided a more confident greening to cloak and insulate the livening. Deer came into the dappled shadows, aurochs and elk as well.

By 6,000–7,000 years ago there were hunters of that Mesolithic sort making use of a coastal territory in the land we know as Denmark, near what would one day be the site of the city of Copenhagen. They would have been drawn to the zone between the land and the sea by the promise of rich pickings. The human population of the whole of Scandinavia then might have numbered in the few thousands at most.

Those people of the fledgling Denmark were in the habit of burying their dead, laid out in graves. The cemetery a few of them created at the place we call Vedbaek was found and excavated in the mid-1970s. A total of seventeen graves were revealed, some oval in shape and some rectangular. The bodies, mostly adult men and women, had been laid down flat on their backs. Most were buried alone but there were two double burials and one triple. Both double graves contained, in each case, a young woman and a newborn baby, buried side by side; the one triple burial was of two adults with a one-year-old child between them. One of the seventeen graves was empty. Most of the dead were accompanied by precious things, precious to them at least – clothing, items made of wood and other organic materials incapable of enduring millennia in the earth. If these burials are works of art, then only those lines most deeply etched have survived. All else has been erased, the colours done away with.

Of all the graves, the example deemed richest is one of the two containing a young woman and a newborn baby together. She was likely around eighteen years old when she died, of cause or causes unknown – young to us, but who can say much, now, about life expectancy then? The baby was newborn at the time of death and had been laid close by the woman's side, on her right and upon a swan's wing. There is no way to be certain of the baby's sex, the bones being too immature, slight and brittle as the quills of the feathers upon which he or she was laid, barely touched by life at all. A long blade of flint, blue-grey, had been laid on top of the little body, diagonally across the hips. When the woman was laid down, her head seemingly rested upon some sort of pillow, maybe a folded item like a dress or some other piece of clothing long since vanished into dust. There were shells near her feet, along with teeth of elk, deer and seal, suggesting she had been clad in a garment decorated with those trinkets. Nearly 200 teeth collected from deer and boar were beside her head, along with perforated snail shells, that together may once have formed the stuff of a necklace.

Beyond those observable facts, all else about her – and about the infant by her side and the rest of the people buried thereabouts – can only be supposition, or imagination. But all the time separating us from them has allowed for a percolation of sorts, or a distillation, so that what remains is strong, potent.

It is easiest to assume they were mother and child, those two, and drowned together in the river of birth. That their remains were treated so kindly suggests grief and love in the hearts of those left behind on its banks, only watching as the current swept loved ones away. If the animal teeth found by her head ever did form a necklace then its baubles were the trophies of a hunter, gathered from the jawbones of prey and set aside for the making of the keepsake. It is also easy to assume that that hunter was hers, theirs – husband to the one and father to the other. Or perhaps he was father and grandfather – father to a daughter and grandfather to his daughter's child. Although the baby seemingly lived only for moments or minutes, a knife was deemed necessary accompaniment. Perhaps the intention was to make plain an inherited status of some sort – declaring to eternity that merely by having been born to that woman, the baby had an elevated rank.

The newborn was given back to the world not lying upon the naked earth but nestled on that white swan's wing. Who does such a thing, thinks of such a thing, except someone who cannot bear the thought of the loved body cold on clay? This wing of a great bird inspires no end of speculation. Maybe the baby's spirit was to be carried aloft, into the heavens. Perhaps those left behind believed that like the migratory birds that leave when their time comes, disappearing beyond the horizon, the infant's spirit, and the mother's, might return to them when the time was right.

We of the twenty-first century try to hold death at bay. We are horrified by the thought, far less the sight, of it. All those thousands of years ago, in Vedbaek, in Denmark, one of the other bodies in the cemetery – that of an adult, but of undetermined sex – had been laid down on a cradle made of red deer antlers. Yet another was furnished with a necklace of more than fifty animal teeth, the jawbone of a pine marten, a small blade of flint and two bones from a roe deer. Here and there in other graves were more keepsakes. Those who grieved evidently saw fit to equip each of their dead for an existence that would continue elsewhere, out of sight. The hunt would go on and the tools of the trade would be needed still. Those who had mattered in one life, borne status, would bear it again in the next.

The Vedbaek cemetery is a rare find, but not unique. There is that long-buried cave in Burrington Combe in Somerset found in the late eighteenth century by two men digging in search of a rabbit – Aveline's Hole. Like the dead in Vedbaek, those who had lain patiently in the darkness beneath the Mendips were accompanied by stone tools, animal teeth and red ochre. Whatever was understood about life after death during the Mesolithic in northern Europe, there were some common strands of thought linking different groups in different places. Confronted by the choice of viewing death as the end or as a mystery, they evidently opted for the latter. Our species has been abroad on the Earth for 200,000 years. There is no reason to believe either our physiology or our mental capacity has altered fundamentally in that time. We and they are the same. It is our circumstances and choices that are different.

In the fourth century BC the Greek philosopher Epicurus could write: 'Death, therefore, the most awful of evils, is nothing to us, seeing that, when we are, death is not come, and, when death is come, we are not.' We have no way of knowing, though, how long ago the same sentiment was first understood and appreciated by our kind. Judging from the graves at Vedbaek and beneath the Mendips it was in a time long before writing of any sort. For 2,000 years Christians believed in life beyond the reach of death. For the last hundred or so, in the time of modern science, we have been telling each other there is no such thing. That this version of events has made us happier in general is debatable at best. Now that we have only our span of years, however brief, death is an empty terror to be held at bay by the pursuit of endless youth. Ten thousand years ago our ancestors imagined spirits carried aloft on the wings of swans. Those hunters made necklaces of the teeth of all the deer that had fed and clad them and imagined an eternity hunting more.

Our ancestors allowed for the hope of something better, or trusted that there was another place where a hunter needed his blade and a person might do well to proclaim their rank and so ensure good treatment. To me, the skeletons of the Vedbaek mother buried with her baby are beautiful beyond adequate description. I feel in my heart the wonder of knowing that love, and the grief that is love's necessary travelling companion, lay waiting to be found in a grave cut thousands of years ago. Untouched, unwearied, those most human of emotions had survived time, just as honey does. Lovelier yet and sweeter is the hope borne on the wing of a swan. It implores us to live in hope.

Birka Girl
and the ones we can't forget

This is the staring, unsleeping eye of the earth;
and what it watches is not our wars.

— ROBINSON JEFFERS,
'The Eye'

IN 2012 I wrote a book and made a television documentary series about the Vikings. As part of it all I visited Lake Mälaren, in west central Sweden, and an island at its heart named Björkö. Like much else in Scandinavia, Mälaren was carved by the action of ice thousands of years ago when the northern hemisphere was colder. Now it is more or less landlocked, and thus a lake, but in the heyday of the Swedish Vikings it was an inlet of the Baltic Sea and suited to their serpentine longships, kicked by oars or blown with wind inhaled by broad sails. By some time in the 700s there was a port town called Birka, on Björkö's north-west side. Modern Swedes have been excavating the place off and on for more than a hundred years, drawn first of all by 3,000 burial mounds spread like a rash beyond the settlement's ancient fortifications, proof of many lives.

So many towns and cities squat like cuckoos upon old nests, earlier traces obscured or tossed out altogether. But for reasons still not understood, Birka was abandoned in the late 900s and left for time to deal with.

No one after the Vikings chose the place for their own, so it has slept for centuries but for the occasional disturbance by archaeologists.

The legacy of Vikings living and dying there left a thick layer of blackened soil, heaped like a blanket and concealing all they left behind. Within the richness, archaeologists have found much evidence of that past time. Birka's residents were jewellers, working in precious metals and polished stones. Other craftspeople cut and shaped leather and fur; yet more used base metals and wood. Birka seems to have been a planned town, laid out in one go. Houses with allotted land, each separated from its neighbour by passages, pathways and ditches. There has been speculation about an all-powerful chief, whose concept Birka was from the beginning. It did well, becoming an important hub for traders bound east to fledgling Russia and south into Europe.

The houses and other buildings were mostly on the lakeside, with allotments of land spreading inland behind, like trailing ribbons. For security, they raised a semi-circle of earthen rampart, penetrated by wooden gates they could keep watch over. There was a stone-built fortress too, for armed guardians. For the most part, access to Birka was via wooden jetties built out into the lake itself, on stilts; a place of the water then, as much as of the land. For many years it seems it was busy with travellers and traders from all over. Archaeologists have found, in graves within the burial mounds, gold and silver from Arabia, silk from Asia and all manner of fine things besides. It was nothing less than an emporium, the air around its jetties thick no doubt with smells of spices, sounds of foreign languages.

Close by the stone fortress, called the Borg, is the site of a burial mound excavated, along with many others, in the nineteenth century. By any estimate it is a prime plot on high ground overlooking the ghosts of the town. It is all but in the shadow of a great block of white stone incorporated into the Borg itself. Since the time of the first excavations the monolith has been regarded as marking a founder's grave – perhaps that of the great chief whose ambition and achievement Birka was.

In the grave, archaeologists found a wooden coffin (its remains at least: wood fragments and rivets of iron) collapsed around and upon the remains of a little girl. The latter-day grave robbers had the wit to appreciate the fragility of what they had found and removed the entirety of the block enfolding her, prior to painstaking work to preserve the bones in safer surroundings. All that remains – all that was revealed – is on display now in a glass case in the Stockholm Museum. There you can see her poor bones, the stumps of her coffin. She was laid down wearing a necklace of twenty-one glass beads, dulled now but surely bright then, and with a gold-plated brooch upon her chest. She had also been provided with a little cylinder carved from bone, a container for needles made of the same, something normally worn only by Viking women who had come of age.

Given the location of her grave, close to the Borg, it is assumed Birka Girl, as she is known, was a person of note; valued, loved. The gilded brooch she wore in life, or that they gave her after death, would have been pinned to her dress, which has long since deteriorated. Since she was so evidently valued, those who have spent time thinking about her since have imagined it was a dress of rich fabric that she wore, of the most expensive colour – which in those days was the crimson red made of the crushed wings of beetles hard to find.

Most affecting of all is the evident slightness of her bones. More than half of Viking children died before the age of ten, of illness or for want of some necessity. Specialists have said Birka Girl was no more than six when she died, of causes unknown. The weight of the earth, coupled with the passage of time, had seen to it that her skull was crushed to fragments. When it was pieced together again it revealed an unexpected face, with a mild deformity. The space between her eyes was wider than usual, likewise the distance separating nose from top lip, suggesting she might have been carried by a mother who drank too much alcohol.

Beside the museum case containing her remains stands a little mannequin, made to give a sense of Birka Girl in life. It is life-size but tiny, almost like a doll, and clad in brightest red. The face is beguiling, unfamiliar in ways hard to pinpoint or express. I found the suggestion of her look haunting, and she has been unforgettable. She often comes to mind. I think of her like a bird, or an ethereal elf-child skipping along a jetty by the lake while sailors unpack strange cargoes from their ships.

From the way she was treated in death, it would seem that in life she was special, unique. I like to think they held her close, her family, like a talisman – their lucky mascot – and that her passing broke their hearts and had them do their very best for her.

I say the little girl in red has haunted me – she has – but I am always pleased to see her when she comes. Like the baby laid down with its mother at Vedbaek, Birka Girl had time only to be lightly touched by life and might have passed through without registering at all. She was unfledged when she fell. But it is that baby and the little girl in red I think of more than warriors or kings. Ephemeral as footsteps in ash or mud, so likely to be washed away, and yet those are the ones that come to mind most often. Those are the ones that have lasted and that have changed me. The loss of such potential, of the chance to experience all that matters in the human universe, is too much to bear and should always be unforgettable.

Like the Vedbaek baby, it is the way Birka Girl was treated by her own that makes her memory immortal. Tiny and otherworldly, she lived and died 1,300 years ago. Her folk buried her in the place of highest honour, in the shadow of the father of their home. That someone so slight, the least of them you might say, was so mourned and missed says a great deal about what matters most about having been alive in the world. By one estimate, the remembering of an individual by others is only four generations deep – which is to say the memory of each one of us dies, at the latest, with our great-grandchildren. Birka Girl is remembered yet, and valued. The least of us, the barest trace we make and without thinking, might matter most of all. To have been loved at all might be everything a person will ever need.

Huanchaquito Las Llamas
and ancient hurt

The features had swollen and begun to liquefy . . .
the face of a young girl disappearing . . . beauty
haunting horror . . . What ideology has that
oozing face for a price? What abstraction is
worth that smell?

– P. J. O'ROURKE,
Holidays in Hell

T O ME, SKELETONS excavated during archaeological digs are not
frightening, not in the least. Mesmerizing proof of life (and death),
they are fellow travellers and never horrifying or sickening. Bare bones
held fast in clay for centuries or millennia have surrendered all their
power to shock, any horror dissolved along with the flesh.

The American journalist P. J. O'Rourke was in the Philippines in
1986 and witnessed some of the chaos that followed the end of the
twenty-one-year regime led by Ferdinand and Imelda Marcos. Cora-
zon Aquino was president by then, but all manner of attempted coups
and other unrest swirled around the islands like bad weather. O'Rourke
watched the exhumation of the body of a twenty-six-year-old pregnant woman who had been shot and killed during one of countless

231

incidents. She had been with the New People's Army (NPA), the soldiers of the Communist Party of the Philippines (CPP), during a clash with government troops. Felled by a stray bullet, she was briefly buried until her family came to recover her body after a few days.

When we find the graves of the ancient dead it is easy to be insulated from any sadness that attended their loss and to be clinical, even romantic, in our response to all that is left behind. Those who loved and mourned them are long gone, taking their grief beyond our reach. Those dead are not ours. It can be hard to accept, even to remember, that they were ever alive. Sometimes skeletons have the look of art installations placed only to amaze and beguile. They can be beautiful. The Vedbaek mother and baby are beautiful to me but their dying tore no hole in the weave of my universe. A newborn baby has 270 bones. Some fuse as the years go by, so that an adult has only 206. This is another work of transformation; young to old. The mother and baby of Vedbaek are an alpha and omega of what it is to be human and alive. As works of engineering, their skeletons are compelling and fascinating. The special things buried alongside are captivating. Excavating the bones of a fellow human being is an intimate act, though the intimacy cuts only one way, the bones and artefacts being raw colours on a palette ready for blending into any picture we want to see. Harder to find and to feel is the pain of loss and the reality of dying. Impossible to see is the horror of wrongful death. An intact skeleton does not preserve desperate struggle, fear, suffering, injustice, cruelty. Archaeologists need reminding of those, from elsewhere. A description like O'Rourke's is therefore important.

Between the tenth and fifteenth centuries, a 600-mile-long swathe of the Pacific coast of what is now Peru was the kingdom of Chimor. The Chimú believed their civilization had been founded by Taycanamo who was born from a golden egg and arrived from the sea. The kingdom's capital city was Chan Chan, at the mouth of the Río Moche near where the modern city of Trujillo sits today. At its peak, Chan Chan amounted to 8 square miles of buildings made of adobe bricks and was home to as many as 40,000 people, more than half of them craftsmen engaged in the production of all manner of high-status treasures. Before the rise of the Inca civilization that swallowed them up, Chimor was the greatest kingdom in Peru.

In 2011, people living in the seaside village of Huanchaquito noticed bones sticking out of the sand on the nearby beach, gradually being eroded by wind and waves. Archaeologists were informed and duly attended the site. What they unearthed were the graves of 140 children. Also buried were the corpses of 200 young llamas – hence the naming of the site as Huanchaquito Las Llamas. Examination of the children's skeletons revealed knife marks across their breast bones and dislocation of their ribcages, suggesting they had been split open for the removal of vital organs, most likely their hearts. It was not possible to know if the cutting and breaking had been the cause of death – hearts excised while beating – or if the eviscerations had been carried out after killing by some other means that left no trace on the bones. Analysis of the skeletons made clear that all of the children had been healthy and well nourished up until their time of death. There were preserved footprints nearby suggesting the children had been walked in procession to the place where they were killed, butchered and buried. Red pigment on skulls and bones showed their faces and bodies had been smeared with the same substance, either in death or in life. All of it was proof of a mass sacrifice around 600 years ago.

This was the custom of *capacocha*, or some variant form. *Capacocha* is Inca and means something like 'solemn sacrifice', but the Inca did not invent it. Human sacrifice, of children as well as adults, was a feature of Meso-American and South American civilization stretching back millennia. Incas, Aztecs and Mayans were all practitioners of the ritualized taking of life – so too the mysterious Olmecs who preceded the rest, rising as a distinct people some time around the end of the second millennium BC.

When the Spaniards marched into South America in the early years of the sixteenth century, the Aztecs were still spreading the shadow of their hand over more and more territory. They had to: expansion was critical. Just as a shark that stops swimming forward might drown, so the Aztec Empire needed to keep moving in search of new conquests in order to keep itself alive. Subject populations were left intact, with their rulers in place. Uprisings were commonplace and almost encouraged. On a whim, the Aztecs could accuse any group of misbehaviour and so re-invade, taking prisoners in the process – prisoners who were fodder for the cult of sacrifice that was central to Aztec thinking. Peace and stability was unthinkable, unworkable. Simmering war was vital; bloody, ritualized death a constant. It was a hard horse to ride, creating for its inhabitants an atmosphere of unceasing tension and anxiety.

When they encountered the Spaniards, the Aztecs' desire to take captives rather than kill the enemy made them vulnerable to defeat by those better armed and willing to annihilate. Also unsettling for the Aztecs was the belief that their civilization had been created by a god who had come and gone long before. He was Quetzalcoatl, with white skin and a beard, and he had departed into the east after promising he would return from the same direction – lending the Spaniards' arrival and appearance the air of a prophecy fulfilled.

The Aztec capital city was Tenochtitlán, on islands in Lake Texcoco joined together by causeways, one of which was 5 miles long. In 2017, archaeologists excavating deep beneath the streets and buildings of Mexico City, which supplanted Tenochtitlán, found 650 human skulls – men, women and children – arranged as the base of a great circular tower. The conquistadors who first encountered Tenochtitlán wrote that for grandeur the city surpassed both Rome and Constantinople. Every bit as great an impression was made on those Spaniards by the edifice the locals called Huey Tzompantli – that great rack made of 20,000 human skulls harvested from the victims of sacrifice. The skulls the archaeologists found formed the lower level of a circular tower within what the Spaniards christened Templo Mayor, the 'great temple'. Inside the pyramidal structure were shrines to several Aztec deities including the sun god Huitzilopochtli and the rain god Tlaloc. Huitzilopochtli was especially thirsty for blood, having gained the taste when other gods of the pantheon sacrificed themselves to him, so that he might have the energy to light up the day.

Astounded first of all by the temples and other buildings of the wondrous city, the sheer scale of it, and then shocked by the trophies made of men, women and children, the conquistadors quickly came to judgement. Appalled by the culture of sacrifice – the flaying alive, the ripping open of the chests of the living, the tearing out of living hearts, the severing and keeping of heads for the making of towers – the incomers found justification for cruelties of their own, and crushed the local way of life. It was only an excuse, but a useful one. Along with much else that drew their ire, Templo Mayor would eventually be levelled and replaced with a cathedral to the Christian God.

Further south, the Spaniards encountered the Inca Empire. By the end of the fifteenth century it sprawled across a vast territory from Ecuador to Chile. Just as the Aztecs had taken control of the older civilization of the Mayans, so the Incas, fledged in the city of Cuzco in the twelfth century, had emerged as cuckoos in the nest of the Chimú. Inca civilization was more sophisticated and more peaceful than that of the Aztecs. Just as rich in gold, silver and copper, the social structures that had evolved in the land of the Inca were based upon the submission of the individual to the state.

Thousands of miles of roads wound their way throughout the domain, even conquering the obstacle posed by the Andes. Relays of runners could carry messages, either verbally or in the form of knots in coloured cords called *quipu*, the length and breadth of the empire in a few days. Every soul, from highest to lowest, knew and accepted his or her place in the grand scheme. Every ounce of gold, every potato and head of corn was owned by the state and distributed by way of a centralized network. Like the Aztecs, Chimú and Mayans, the Incas never discovered the wheel and cargo was moved by caravans of llamas, the species that formed the backbone of the entire civilization.

When the Spanish heard the word *Inka* they understood it to mean all the people in the civilization. In fact Inka was a ruler, or one of the ruling class of perhaps 40,000 people out of a population of several million. Individuals owed the Inka and the state the sweat of their brows and the strength of their backs – a compulsory service called *mita*. Sophisticated organizational skills and the effort of a supine population made possible farming not just of valley floors, but on terraces cut into even the most precipitous slopes. They were architects and builders of astonishing ability and ambition, their fortresses and aqueducts still testament to their prowess. Inca civilization was hive mentality by any other name.

Supreme among the ruling class was the despotic Sapa Inka – the only Inca. Child sacrifice among those people was ordered by the Sapa Inka. Victims were selected from all over the empire on the basis of their beauty and physical perfection. Only the best, the loveliest, unblemished virgins, were fit for the gods. Having been assembled in the capital, the children – some just babies and toddlers – were walked or carried to places of sacrifice. Those too young for solid food were suckled at their mother's breasts to ensure they remained healthy, and peaceful. Each sacrifice was dispatched in one of four ways – by strangulation, suffocation, burial alive or with a blow to the head. Often the shrines were high in the mountains, where conditions sometimes mummified the remains for discovery in the modern era. At an altitude of 22,000 feet on the Argentinian volcano Llullaillaco, three such sad, shaming treasures were recovered in 1999. Two girls – one aged fifteen, one perhaps half that age – and a boy of about six or seven were found so perfectly preserved they might have been sleeping. Only time has muffled and disguised the horror of their murders.

The Spaniards and the rest of the Europeans who first encountered the civilizations of Meso-America and South America were distracted at all times by gold and their artful finery. Like perfume slathered on a corpse, it could not cover the stink of the heartlessness of it all. For despite the gold it was an ugly world, founded upon brutal disregard for human life and a preoccupation with death. Human sacrifice had been practised elsewhere, and throughout history, but not on the scale witnessed in the Americas. It was demanded and made possible by a determination to sacrifice, in every sense of the word, the individual to the presumed greater good of the state.

Within the reach of living memory we have lived alongside ideologies that had (and have) no qualms about slaughtering the millions in pursuit of Utopia. The Soviet Union of Lenin and Stalin oversaw the deaths of at least 50 million people in the twentieth century. Mao Tse-tung's Great Leap Forward accounted for perhaps 100 million more. Then there was the North Korea of the Kims, Cambodia under Pol Pot. When ideologues lead the way to a promised land existing only in their imaginations, favouring the group above the individual, the path they make is a corduroy road of uncounted corpses laid one after the other.

I have been in awe of the distant dead, struck dumb by the tenant of this grave or that. I have peeled clay from foreheads and chins, scooped it from empty eye sockets, and only wondered what they ever saw. I have failed to think of suffering. Now I look back and wonder what I missed, what I was unable to discern among the wrappings of the gift. Now I understand that the ancient dead might be read as warnings too. Although they may be muffled by time – and we might not want to hear them, see them – pain and suffering are always with us. We owe it to the dead to know that just as love survives in the ground, so too does evidence of evil.

237

12.

Sacrifice

The Dying God
and the sacred oak

The oak was the mighty giant, who held the ball
moon in goblet fingers.

JOHN LEWIS-STEMPEL,
The Glorious Life of the Oak

BALDR WAS A Norse god, one of All-Father Odin's many sons. It may be that all the male gods were Odin's sons but Baldr was the favourite – warmest, wisest and loveliest of all, a shining star. In the so-called *Prose Edda*, written in the thirteenth century by Icelandic historian Snorri Sturluson, Baldr is plagued by dreams of imminent death. He unburdens to his mother, the goddess Frigg, who in turn asks all animals, birds and plants, all metals and elements, all objects – everything in heaven and Earth – to swear they will never harm him. They duly promise; all except the mistletoe, which she deems too young to ask, and which is in any case from a land too far away to matter.

It soon becomes the preferred pastime of the gods to gather round Baldr and throw at him anything they can lay hands on. They laugh as every missile bounces off, leaving him unhurt. Only Loki, maker of mischief, is displeased and goes to Frigg disguised as a woman. He tricks her into telling him about the mistletoe. Loki travels until he finds an oak tree. He takes some mistletoe from among its branches and from it fashions an arrow. Returning to where the gods are once again at their game with Baldr, Loki approaches the blind god Hodr who has so far taken no part in the game. With Loki guiding his arm, Hodr shoots the arrow at Baldr and pierces him through and kills him.

For the gods, the death of Baldr is the worst of times. Of course he is honoured with a fine funeral. His body is carried down to the shore where lies his ship, *Hringhorni*, greatest of all vessels. His body is laid upon its deck and the gods seek to launch it so they can set it on fire to consume the body. *Hringhorni* is too heavy and so they ask the giant Hyrrokkin to help. She rides to their aid on a gigantic wolf she controls with living snakes for reins and kicks the ship so hard the speed of its passing into the water sets fire to its rollers. When Baldr's wife, Nanna, sees him laid on his pyre, aboard the ship, she dies of grief. The gods place her body next to that of her husband, along with his horse and all its trappings. Odin goes aboard and stoops and whispers something in Baldr's ear. Ever since that moment gods and men have wondered what it was the All-Father said then to his dead son. I think he said 'I love you'. What else is there, in the end?

Another of Odin's sons, Hermodr, is sent to the underworld to ask the goddess Hel (a name that means 'hidden', the person and the place) to give Baldr back to the living world. If all things on Earth will weep for him, she says, then Baldr may return to the world above. All comply; all weep salty tears except a giantess called Thokk who remains unmoved. Maybe Thokk was Loki in disguise, but it mattered not, and Baldr remained in the world of the dead, awaiting Ragnarök, the end of the world, like all the rest.

By the time Snorri Sturluson recorded his version of the legend in the 1200s, the death of Baldr was already an ancient story. We cannot know how old. Like so many stories it is older than writing, so that some or other version of it had been remembered and recounted. The Russian linguist Anatoly Liberman has suggested that by Snorri's time, whatever had been the original story was infected by contact with the world beyond Iceland and Scandinavia. For one thing mistletoe, one of a class of parasitic plants that draw water and nutrients from a host plant, was a rarity in Snorri's world. It may have been a late addition to the tale, born of contact by his time with somewhere like the British Isles, where the plant is common.

In *The Golden Bough*, the Scottish anthropologist J. G. Frazer described how, in the minds of the ancients, mistletoe was imbued with magical properties. Since it never touched earth, remaining suspended between earth and sky in the branches of the oak tree, it was an object of fascination. Where did it come from? How did it get into the tree? How did it live? The oak was deciduous and shed its leaves in winter. During that time, when the tree was mostly dead, or just asleep, the mistletoe remained green. It may have seemed that the still-beating heart of the tree was in that evergreen tangled in its branches. Of all the trees in the wood, the oak was the one most often struck by lightning. The ancients observed as much and imagined some special relationship between the sky – or a deity in the sky – and the oak. Did the spirit or god of lightning favour the oak, and so reach out to it more frequently? Perhaps the power of sun and lightning was stored inside that most special, favourite tree, waiting to be set free by men.

Fire might be made by rubbing together sticks of many different species, but in ancient minds combustion was most imminent in the wood of the oak. If an animal spirit might be summoned by an artist from the rock of a cave, so fire was closest to the surface of that wood and readiest for coaxing. They believed that fire was stored inside the tree, waiting to be released for the benefit of all. According to Frazer it followed that mistletoe, a passenger of the oak in particular, was understood as a manifestation of that union between sun, lightning and the tree – the legacy of lightning bolts. So the oak tree was venerated above all, becoming sacred to druids among others. Whoever they were, the druids took their name from those trees. The proto-Indo-European roots of the word are *deru*, meaning 'oak', and *weid*, meaning 'see' or 'know' – hence druids were those who saw and knew (as in understood) the oak.

The story of Baldr's death may have been made more complicated over time, twisted like the limb of an aged oak as it accommodated, grew around, more and more ideas. According to Liberman the original version was simpler. He has suggested it was about two spirits, or gods – one shining bright in the world above, the other dark in the world below. Like good and bad, order and chaos, yin and yang, they coexisted side by side, one the opposite of the other. Baldr was illuminated while Hodr could not or would not see. Baldr protected life, including some or other plant that was especially sacred to him. Hodr was jealous of all that he lacked, all that he was not. Without any interference by Loki, Hodr it was who learned the name of the sacred plant from Baldr's mother, found it and fashioned from it a weapon with which he killed his half-brother. His mother mourned and asked for his return, but to no avail. This is a mother's lot; every mother gives birth despite knowing her child must die in the end. Come what may, her child will be sacrificed to the inevitable. The child will sometimes be happy and healthy, but will die sooner or later. This is the sacrifice every mother makes, knowingly and bravely.

For as long as our species has been conscious and in the business of remembering, we have told each other stories to make sense of life and death. Cain and Abel; Alpha et Omega. All around the world there are stories of gods – forms like us but better, brighter, closer to heaven and perfection. Gods of light resist the darkness, the chaos, and bring about order. Always the darkness lies in wait, ready to swallow the light. Fire is part of stories from the beginning. Fire is given, won, or stolen from the sky, the sun, the lightning. Mastery of fire ensures life – life for the crops, for the animals, for the people – and also the purification of all that is unclean.

Among the Aztecs – who walked their children into the mountains or to the sea, or carried them in their arms, and butchered them to keep the darkness at bay – there was the story of the god Quetzalcoatl, born to a virgin. He had a twin brother, Xolotl, who was the evening star, among other things. Quetzalcoatl was the god of light, and also justice, mercy and the wind. One night a fellow god, Tezcatlipoca, got Quetzalcoatl drunk on fermented agave. In his inebriated state he raped his celibate sister. In the morning he was so ashamed he set himself on fire. His heart rose into the sky with his ashes and became the morning star. No matter how bright the fire, darkness is there too.

In his book *The Gulag Archipelago*, Aleksandr Solzhenitsyn wrote, 'the line dividing good and evil cuts through the heart of every human being. And who is willing to destroy a piece of his own heart?' The Aztecs tried, even cutting out the hearts of their own children, and no good came of it. They are hardly alone. The human story drips with blood – of the innocent and the guilty both. A single candle casts a shadow. Good is there in the devil and the devil is there in the good, in God.

According to J. G. Frazer, Baldr was the very spirit of the oak tree. His life force, his soul, was in the mistletoe. Just as the dark wizard Voldemort in J. K. Rowling's imagined universe was vulnerable to the destruction of his horcruxes – objects in which he had hidden fragments of his soul – so Baldr could be killed by a weapon made of mistletoe wherein his life force lay. As a god he was immortal, and almost invulnerable – but not quite.

For the longest time our species has sought understanding. Early on, it seems there was an appreciation that life was hard and that the natural world posed endless challenges. There would be pain and suffering. In the end there would be death. Happiness could only ever be fleeting. It was important to accept this – to accept that humanity was subject to the same powers that challenged all life. It is our consciousness that has imbued the universe with meaning; made plain to us our awful predicament. The stories that suggested themselves to our ancestors were told and retold. Over time, layers formed around the central point – like the nacre around a grain of sand that makes a pearl. The hard grain of truth became hard to see, obscured by opalescence.

We are vulnerable and finite. Achilles, greatest of the Greek warriors, hero of the siege of Troy, was born to a goddess and a mortal king. His mother, the sea nymph Thetis, held him by one ankle and dipped him in the River Styx to make him invulnerable to hurt – every loving mother's wish for her child. But one heel, where she had held him, was untouched by the water and so remained weak. This was the spot Paris found with his arrow, ending Achilles. Mary gave birth to Jesus, God made flesh. Even she would not be spared the ultimate loss. Even knowing what he knew – that he was God and heaven-bound – Jesus still had moments on the cross he could not bear. 'Why hast thou forsaken me?' he asked. Life is so hard even a god – God – cannot bear every moment of it.

Our lives are forfeit, a debt that will be repaid willingly or not. We are all sacrificed. The stories tell us so. Even gods die.

246

forehead, they deduced it was a body laid down long ago. When they arrived at the scene they brought with them people from the Silkeborg Museum, who might know best.

The body was curled as one sleeping, on its side. Naked except for a cap of leather and a belt of hide around his waist, he was stained the same black-bronze as the surrounding peat, and shining; around his neck was a noose of plaited leather drawn tight and coiled snakelike over one shoulder (a fallen man and a serpent in the frame). He was perfectly preserved so that his witnesses could testify to close-cropped hair, stained ginger, on his head beneath his cap and fine stubble on his chin. Here was the victim of an ancient crime, if crime it was. A grown man and not a boy throttled with a noose. Satisfied it was hardly within their jurisdiction, the police deferred to the museum staff who sent word to one Peter Glob (P. V. Glob as he is better known), archaeologist at Copenhagen Museum. He came and christened the foundling Tollund Man.

Exhumed, he was a marvel, a sleeping time traveller, and burnished as though cast from a mould. Acidic tannins in the peat had worked on his flesh – a pickling to keep him through the long night to come. Sealed beyond the reach of the elegant processes of decomposition he was quite intact. X-rays revealed liver, lungs, heart and all. Inside his stomach was a last meal, undigested – a porridge of many seeds, both wild and cultivated: barley, bristlegrass, camomile, gold-of-pleasure, knotweed, linseed. Archaeologists have suggested some of the gruel's ingredients, at least forty different ones, would have been hard to come by all at the same time, and must have been from stores set aside for special occasions. The same natural magic that had preserved Tollund Man's flesh had taken a toll on his bones, decalcifying them. (In other times and places bog bodies have been found that are mere sacks of flesh, the skeleton within dissolved completely.) This made it hard to know if his neck had been broken by hanging from the noose, or if the life had been choked out of him where he stood, or knelt, or lay,

248

another's knee hard against his back for leverage. He had swallowed his own tongue. Despite the misery, the cruelty of his dispatching, his body had been handled kindly afterwards. Rather than casually cast aside – flung into a ditch as it were – he had been placed with care.

Once Glob had had him lifted clear he saw that his man had lain upon a layer of moss of the sort that grew on Danish bogs two millennia before; he had been lying there, being swallowed whole, since the Iron Age. (Later, measurements of the radioactive carbon in his carroty stubble showed that he lived and died in the late fifth or early fourth century before the birth of Christ.) His wisdom teeth were fully grown through his tanned gums, so while it was hard to say how old he had been at death, he was at least an adult man.

At the time of his discovery it was not possible to keep the whole of him. His earthly womb had stopped time dead, but once pulled from it the clock began again, and so too his corruption. Only his head was treated therefore, with polyethylene glycol (it was all the conservators had), while a clever replica was made of the rest. It is this composite, the real and the fake brought seamlessly together, that is on display in Silkeborg. Above all else it is that head, that face, that is the miracle that holds the gaze harder than any Mona Lisa smile. Furrowed forehead, heavy-lidded eyes, bottom lip pouting as though mulling over a thought. If he died in pain or fear there is no hint of either. His peace is unnerving. He seems ready to wake at the snapping of fingers.

Two years later, near the village of Grauballe in Jutland, more peat cutting revealed another bog body. Glob was quickly on the scene again, and rather than dig the truffle up there and then he had so-called Grauballe Man moved to a lab while still locked, iron-lung-like, inside his block of peat. Once exposed and investigated the whole corpse was carefully tanned to leather and stuffed with bark to keep its shape. He too, poor soul, had been put to death 2,500 years before, his throat slit from ear to ear with a sharp edge.

Tollund Man and Grauballe Man were hardly the first, far less the only, bog bodies. In 1938, and just 200 feet from where Tollund Man was later found, the remains of Elling Woman had been unearthed. Less well preserved, her corpse had been wrapped post-mortem in a sheep-skin and so was mistaken for a drowned animal by the farmer who found her. Glob had her as a *man* in his book, *The Bog People*, though long hair carefully plaited might have suggested otherwise. It took an X-ray of her pelvis to reveal the truth. There has been speculation she was put to death at the same time as Tollund Man. She too had been hanged or strangled.

There have been more. No doubt for as long as folk have cut into blanket peat (for fuel, or for preserved timber – the so-called 'bog oak' that is prized where living trees are absent) there have been discoveries of preserved bodies, and yarns spun to explain them. Only in the mod-ern era, though, have the techniques existed properly to investigate and then conserve them for posterity. They are more of Earth's memories, fixed like shrimps in aspic.*

Best guesses have Tollund Man sacrificed to Nerthus, an earth god-dess worshipped by pagans in ancient times in parts of north-east Europe. Glob had read about Nerthus in *Germania*, by the Roman author Tacitus. For all the life she gave, she took. Some representation of her was kept hidden, wrapped in a sheet, and on the back of a wagon drawn by young cows that had not yet calved. The wagon rested in a sacred grove on an island but travelled from time to time. Wherever she went there could be no war, only celebration. On the wagon's return to the island and the grove it was washed by slaves who were then drowned in her honour.

Those faithful to Nerthus had it that she embodied spring, and every

---

* In the frozen northern latitudes, the lands crisped by permafrost, all manner of animals have been found intact, but icebound. When mammoth carcasses come to light the scientists must race against time – not for fear of the defrosting but because 10,000-year-old mammoth meat is a delicacy soon devoured by the locals.

year required a mortal man to couple with and so bring forth from the earth new life. It seemed Tollund Man might have been selected for the role. Perhaps he was high-born, of a caste to the liking of a goddess. Or maybe he was a criminal, a guilty man, his execution doubling as the necessary sacrifice. Maybe Elling Woman was Eve to his Adam, the luckless pair of them dangled out of Eden on lengths of leather rope.

I first learned about Tollund Man in the poem of that name by Nobel Prize-winning Irish poet Seamus Heaney. He wrote and spoke about having seen things other than human bodies preserved. Country folk were in the habit of burying stores of butter in the peat, knowing it would last better there than in the air above. As he noted in 'Bogland', neighbours of his had dug up the skeleton of a megaloceros, the same species of gigantic deer that was known to the artists of the cave at Chauvet:

> They've taken the skeleton
> Of the Great Irish Elk
> Out of the peat, set it up
> An astounding crate full of air.

In his imagination and in his writing, Heaney returned over and over to the bogs and the bodies. During the 1970s and the Troubles he saw sad parallels between the old and newly dead. Nerthus, the goddess, had demanded blood sacrifices in Denmark, Germany and elsewhere; Ireland, another motherland, was claiming more of the same from the tenants of the modern world. In 'Tollund Man', Heaney wished that the ground made holy and fertile by ancient pagan sacrifice might cause life to 'germinate' and so bring victims of sectarian murder back from the dead. As a Roman Catholic he wondered, worried even, that such a wish might make him guilty of blasphemy. He had known of an atrocity committed by Protestants against four Catholic brothers in the

1920s. The executioners of Tollund Man had treated his remains with reverence, preferring to see and think of him asleep. He had been fed a last meal of all the bounty of the bog and the fields about. He had been harvested. Given that he was a gift for the goddess his still-warm self had likely been carried to some meaningful spot and carefully put away for ever. The killers of the young Catholic brothers had dragged their bodies, alive or dead, along a railway line,

> Tell-tale skin and teeth
> Flecking the sleepers . . .

Seamus Heaney is gone now. I met him the year before he died, to hear him talk about the poetry of Robert Burns. We had tea and home-cooked scones and I was in awe. As well as Burns he talked about home and childhood and the ever-presence of the past.

Tollund Man the poem and the person are reminders that there have always been those ready to make their point by killing others. Only time has taken the sting out of the deaths of Elling Woman, Tollund Man, Grauballe Man and the rest of those sacrificed in ancient times. They are treasures now of sorts, and silent, but it is 6 feet of peat that muffles any screaming they made, that has absorbed their tears and their pissing in fear. The wonder of their accidental preservation, the acid in the tannin, only sanitizes and should not erase the reality of the acts that ended them.

Sacrifice is surrendering to God, to the future, something that is precious now. The hope is that God and/or the future will be kind in return. We take the future for granted but long ago its existence had to occur to someone for the first time – the notion of a world that did not yet exist but that was somehow on its way. By making sacrifices now, that malleable future world might be moulded into a desirable, compliant shape. Food might be sacrificed, burnt as an offering; so too weapons, tools, jewellery. Eventually it occurred to someone that fellow human beings might be offered up best of all – in effigy or in the flesh.

Humans are still being sacrificed every day, for someone's idea of a more desirable future. In my lifetime, in Heaney's, there were thousands of victims in Ireland, both sides in a civil war convinced of the powerful magic of spilling blood. It is all around us now, in one God-forsaken territory after another. Blood sacrifice in the name of a better future. Only the dead like Tollund Man have seen the end of it. All we seem to have learned so far is that such killing never ends, never will.

> Out here in Jutland
> In the old man-killing parishes
> I will feel lost,
> Unhappy and at home.

Star Carr
and the call of the wild

When the long winter nights come on and the
wolves follow their meat into the lower valleys, he
may be seen running at the head of the pack
through the pale moonlight or glimmering
borealis, leaping gigantic above his fellows, his
great throat a-bellow as he sings the song of the
younger world, which is the song of the pack.

— JACK LONDON,
The Call of the Wild

I ONCE HUNTED CROCODILES in Arnhem Land in north-east
Australia. It is truer to say I was in the boat when a crocodile was
spotted, betrayed by eyes made amber bright in the dark of night by a
powerful torch; I was close when it was harpooned and hauled aboard,
several feet of frightened thrashing muscle, and on the riverbank when
it was killed and cooked on an open fire. People say crocodile tastes like
chicken. In fact chickens and crocodiles taste similar because they are
among the animals alive today that are directly descended from dinosaurs. When a person says crocodile tastes like chicken, what they are
saying, without knowing it, is that both taste like dinosaur.

The hunting of crocodiles, and other fauna, was banned in Queensland in 1974. By then the saltwater crocodile population was in a parlous state, cut to a level that threatened their survival. The Aboriginal elder I was with, Murrandoo Yanner, took evident pleasure in telling me that the big males that survived that period were wily, had learned to stay out of sight ever since. Already huge in 1974, they had grown bigger still. I was reliably informed there were monsters out there on Yanner's patch – hundred-year-old crocodiles up to 30 feet long.

Our hunt, however, was legal. Yanner, courtesy of a landmark ruling in Australia's High Court in 1999, had regained the right of Aboriginal people to do what their ancestors had done – hunt, kill and eat crocodiles. He killed the beast by cutting off its head with a boning knife. More than the blood, I remember clear liquid spurting from its neck, pulsing from some severed crocodilian plumbing. I did not care to ask what it was – some of the nature of crocodile life. Half an hour after the decapitation its jaws still snapped shut when a stick was poked into its mouth, and then opened again.

Aside from a bit of fishing, this has been the limit of my hunting. A friend of mine went on a stag hunt years ago – one of those that form part of the management of a herd, the culling of the elderly and infirm. After hours of stalking, the gamekeeper fired the fatal shot and the beast fell. When it came to the *gralloch*, which is the Gaelic for the necessary disembowelling of the still-warm body, my friend was leaning close over the split carcass when it was pointed out that the stag's heart was absent. The gamekeeper nodded and explained that the velocity of the shot, coupled with pinpoint accuracy, had seen the bullet take the organ with it, in its entirety, out through the exit wound. Truly, dead before it hit the ground. Such is the nature of the modern hunt – instantaneous death delivered from hundreds of yards away.

Murrandoo Yanner had made a determined, stubborn return to the original ways of his ancestors. Disenchanted by much of the modern world and its baleful influence on his clan, and all Aboriginal clans, he had picked up hunting and gathering ways again. His passion for the potential was so intense it was almost fury. His eyes blazed and I was almost afraid of him.

The day before the crocodile hunt, we took a helicopter ride together, looking down on his clanlands as gods might. He had spoken repeatedly about spirit animals and I asked him if such a thing belonged only to Aboriginal people. He said no, that even a Scot like me had a guiding companion in the animal kingdom. He said my mother would have had some kind of meaningful interaction with an animal while pregnant with me, and that that would be my fellow traveller. I said it was too late now to remember or to know. He shrugged.

'Or the universe tells you some other way,' he said.

The words were barely out of his mouth when the pilot, another Aboriginal man, reached back and tapped Yanner's shoulder. He pointed out of the helicopter, down to a sheltered inlet below. A pair of dark shapes, dolphins, were swimming together in a tight circle like the astrological symbol for Pisces, corralling fish prior to gobbling them up.

'Have you ever seen dolphins there before, so far upriver?' the pilot asked Yanner.

'Never in my life,' he replied. 'Never.'

He turned to me.

'There you go, Neil,' he said. 'You asked, and the universe answered.'

His hunting and killing of the crocodile was different from the shooting of the stag my friend witnessed. Rather than with a rifle from far away it was accomplished by having the boat drift to within a man's length of the creature before a harpoon was thrust into its back just below the neck. As it was hauled aboard it made plain it did not appreciate the treatment meted out. The killing on the riverbank was by silent strokes of a long knife and we all watched it die without a sound.

It is hard to imagine how most of us urbanites in the west could be any further removed from the hunt. Farm animals are raised and slaughtered out of sight, their meat presented bloodless, shrink-wrapped and utterly divorced from the reality of living things. Who handles warm guts any more? Few cook and eat them, so recognizable are livers and lungs, kidneys and hearts, sweetbreads and tripe – so inconveniently, unmistakably animal. But if we do not see death, we are made colder towards life, less in awe.

The best part of 12,000 years ago, when the ice was in retreat and the first of the trees – aspen, birch and willow – were taking root in newly made soil, a wide, shallow lake in the territory we know as Yorkshire attracted the attentions of hunters. Formed in a hollow made and left by the ice, no doubt it offered rich pickings – fish, birds and small game. The lake, known to geologists as Flixton, also drew herds of red deer.

Lake Flixton dried up thousands of years ago. Where there had been water, blanket peat grew instead. This change of circumstances has been a boon to archaeologists, the anaerobic peat preserving all manner of organic material. The same conditions, more or less, that stopped time for Tollund Man and the rest of the bog bodies laid up a rich store of the kinds of Mesolithic artefacts that hardly ever survive the millennia. Things made of bone, antlers, wood – all of it has been lying in wait, excavated since just after the end of the Second World War. This is the site called Star Carr, the most important Mesolithic site in Britain.

Star Carr's hunters paid special attention to the red deer. From the antlers they fashioned hundreds of barbed points, like harpoons. Archaeologists have suggested they made more of these points than could ever have been needed for the hunt. To some degree it seems it was the act of making that mattered – antler transformed. That so many found their way into the shallows of the lake suggests not accidental loss but hunters offering up things they valued and needed. Sacrifice.

Best of all, and most captivating: the hunters made themselves antler headdresses. In some of the literature these are called frontlets. The

making of each was a test of patience, skill and hard work. Red deer antler is astonishingly tough. Even the sharpest steel blade makes little
impression and ingenuity is required. To cut through an antler it must
first be bound with cord, which can be set alight and burnt to make
inroads on the material, weakening it ready for snapping. A hunter
wanting a headdress would take an adult male deer in autumn, before
the natural shedding of the antlers. The whole severed head may have
been placed on a fire to cook the flesh and brain for eating. Stone tools
were used to separate that portion of the skull with the antlers attached
and then part of the inner surface of bone was scraped away to reduce
the weight and make it thinner. Much of the weight of the crown of tines
was also removed, presumably to make the finished piece less unwieldy.
Two eyeholes were cut and bored through the mask of bone, and other
perforations made so the headdress could be fixed in place on a hunter's
head with chinstraps. Debate has been endless about whether the headdresses were camouflage for stalking deer, part of the garb for rituals in
which a shaman was transformed into a hybrid man-stag, or both.

The rest of the antler was used for those barbed points, tools for
hunting and fishing. The preponderance of antler tools at Star Carr
makes plain that those hunters were especially focused on that one
beast; fixated even. Maybe the red deer was the spirit animal not just of
one hunter but of them all.

During the late 1940s and early 1950s, twenty-one headdresses were
found at Star Carr. Others have been recovered from the peat in the
years since. They are frightening to me, reminders of stories and figures that scared me as a child: *The Wild Hunt of Hagworthy*, Herne the
Hunter – thoughts of being chased through the dark by horned creatures that are men and yet not. However the headdresses were used,
what matters most is the notion of transformation. Boundaries were
porous and natures less than fixed, or so it seemed. The artists of Chauvet sensed the animal within the rock and sought to bring it to the
surface where it might be outlined and known. Hunters making

headdresses knew the spirit of the deer was in the bone and antler. People were immersed in the natural world, like fish in water. Hunters breathed nature. Fewer and fewer of us sense that connection. We would do well now to pay attention to those who remember the way, or have rediscovered it.

When I was a local newspaper reporter twenty-five years ago, our beat covered the East Lothian town of Dunbar, birthplace of John Muir. Townsfolk there were proud of their connection to the man widely credited in the USA as the father of conservation and the National Parks movement. In 2012 I retraced some of his footsteps, to Yosemite and the High Sierra of California. Muir's father Daniel was a devout Christian and Dunbar fell short of the religious purity he sought. In 1849 he moved his whole family, wife, sons and daughters, to Wisconsin. Young John, just eleven years old, was transfixed by the wild world he found there. Later he studied botany and geology at the University of Wisconsin, although he never graduated.

When he was twenty-nine, and working in a factory making wheels for wagons, he had cause to try to tighten a canvas belt driving a wood saw. The tool he was holding slipped and punctured one of his eyes, the aqueous humour puddling in his cupped hand – a little lake after a cataclysmic event. By the time he made it back to his lodgings the shock of the injury had caused the sight to fail in his undamaged eye as well, so that he was blind. After weeks in a darkened room, the gift of sight returned to both eyes. As far as John was concerned it was a miracle, a divine gift. He decided there and then to see as much as possible of the world, for fear the darkness might descend again.

Years of wandering followed, a life lived as much as possible outdoors and in all weathers. Yosemite struck him hardest of all, baptizing him with something older than his father's brand of Christianity. For months and years he wandered in the wilderness – day and night climbing cliffs and peaks, wondering at the plants and animals. In the midst of a storm he climbed a pine tree, to better feel the force of the tempest. He climbed a cliff, inched along a narrow ledge on its face and stepped behind a waterfall so as to see the full moon through the torrent. Alone and in hobnailed boots he summited peaks over 10,000 feet high. A coat was too much to carry, so he did without. During the day he gathered pinecones, and as darkness fell he would make a fire of them and curl around it for warmth, like a moon around a sun. He wrote books and articles for magazines, awakening his readers to the plight of a natural world under threat from industry and modern agriculture. He had seen beyond the rigid religion of his father to preach a gospel of his own about the rightful place of humankind as only a part of miraculous nature. Perhaps more than by anything else he was captivated by the giant sequoia trees, those great sentinels. When he arrived in Yosemite they were being felled for lumber – a largely pointless enterprise, since the tannin-rich timber generally shattered into matchwood when those giants hit the ground. Convinced of the essential wrongness of cutting down living things that were thousands of years old, some of them older than Christianity, or Islam, or Buddhism, Muir successfully campaigned to have them spared for all time.

'The King tree and me have sworn eternal love, sworn it without swearing,' he wrote in a letter to his friend Jeanne Carr, wife of Dr Ezra Carr, one of his old teachers at university. 'I've taken the sacrament, drank Sequoia wine, Sequoia blood . . . Seen with sunbeams in it, its colour is the most royal of all purples. I wish I was so drunk and Sequoical I could preach the green brown woods to all the juiceless world, descending from this divine wilderness like a John Baptist.'

John Muir was a modern-day prophet. Only quite recently remembered in his homeland of Scotland, he has long been revered in the USA as a father of much that is good. A giant likeness of his bearded face would sit well on Mount Rushmore, purer of spirit than any president.

Better than most, John understood our place in the world, the cosmos. He knew he was a tiny cog in a grand machine and that obeisance before its grandeur might lift him up. Inside the cover of the field journal he carried everywhere on his belt he had written his address as he saw fit: 'John Muir, Earth – planet, universe'. Like a shaman he sensed he was not nature's master, but its supplicant.

In the Cave of the Trois-Frères, in Montesquieu-Avantès in the Ariège of south-west France, there is another torrent of animals frozen long ago. Mammoths, bears, horses, ibex, stags, bison, reindeer – scores of them, and overlying one another, on the walls of a chamber called the Sanctuary. A mad jumble of exuberance, a dizzying cloud of life. The three brothers in question – Jacques, Louis and Max, sons of Count Henri Begouën – were the first to explore the cave in the modern era, two years before the outbreak of the Great War. High above all, out of reach, is the figure called the Sorcerer. First copied and studied (and named) by Henri Breuil, a Catholic priest, it is a strange and other-worldly creation, with the body of a deer and the head of a bearded man. Breuil saw, and so depicted, the antlers of a stag on it as well. From a dozen feet above the floor of the chamber the Sorcerer holds sway, leaping gigantic above his fellows.

The art in the Sanctuary is 15,000 years old and yet still raises goose-bumps on twenty-first-century flesh. It was conjured into being by the same thinking that would later fire the imaginations of the hunters at Star Carr. Beneath the thin silk of modernity we are hunters still. Pulsing in the arteries of our species is our lifeblood, the most royal of all purples and Sequoical. It is wisdom, ancient wisdom. It has flowed from the beginning with the power to refresh and to renew. It is all our ancestors learned and knew, and underneath it all, deep inside our modern selves, we know it too. We eat crocodiles and chickens and know, without knowing it, that both taste like dinosaurs. We know this without knowing because the stuff of us is older than dinosaurs, much older. Coiled in our chemistry, in our DNA, are relics of billions of years of lives lived. That life flows from the younger world, and when we close our eyes in the dark, we can feel it.

Acknowledgements

I have never had much truck with the notion of it taking a village to raise a child, but I do know it takes more than just an author to make a book.

Being steered through the process of transformation – from the error-strewn typescript to the finished piece in all its glory on the bookshelf – is nothing less than humbling. To those who have the eye, the skill, the experience, the patience and the wisdom to do what is necessary, I doff my metaphorical hat.

I had the great good fortune to be looked after by the wonderful team at Transworld: Susanna Wadeson, Helena Gonda, Katrina Whone and Dan Balado took painstaking care of the text and the copyedit. Beci Kelly and Andrew Davidson conjured the cover and illustrations into being. Production was by Cat Hillerton, marketing by Ella Horne and publicity by Tom Hill. A thousand thanks to each in turn.

A thousand thanks also to my literary agent, Eugenie Furniss at 42, and my TV agent Sophie Laurimore at the Soho Agency.

Lastly, to my wife Trudi and our children, Evie, Archie and Teddy, love and deepest gratitude always.

Index

INDEX

ABOUT THE AUTHOR

Neil Oliver was born in Renfrewshire in Scotland. He studied archaeology at the University of Glasgow and worked as an archaeologist before training as a journalist. In 2002 he made his television debut presenting BBC2's *Two Men in a Trench*, in which he and Tony Pollard visited historic British battlefields.

Since then he has been a regular on TV, presenting *A History of Scotland*, *Vikings* and *Coast*. He was appointed President of the National Trust in Scotland in 2017. He travels all the time, but his home is in Stirling, with his wife, three children and an Irish wolfhound.